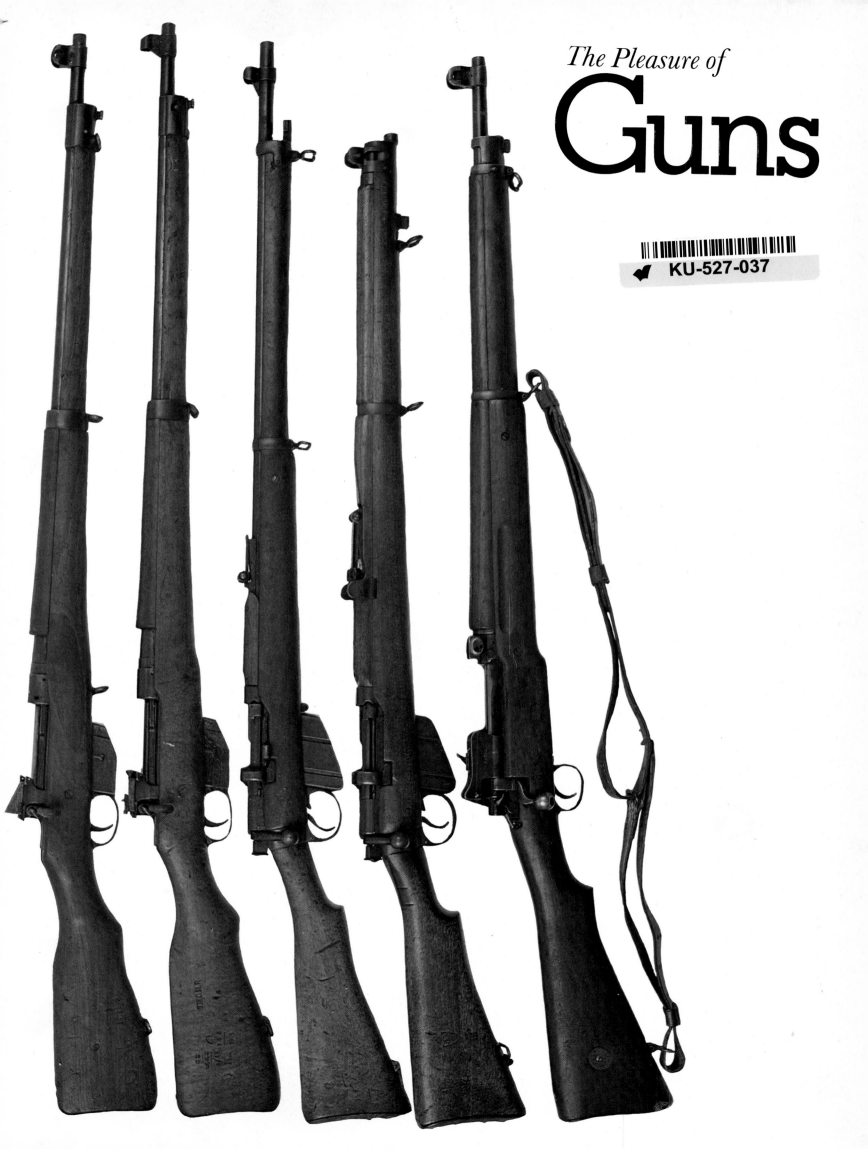

The Pleasure of
Guns

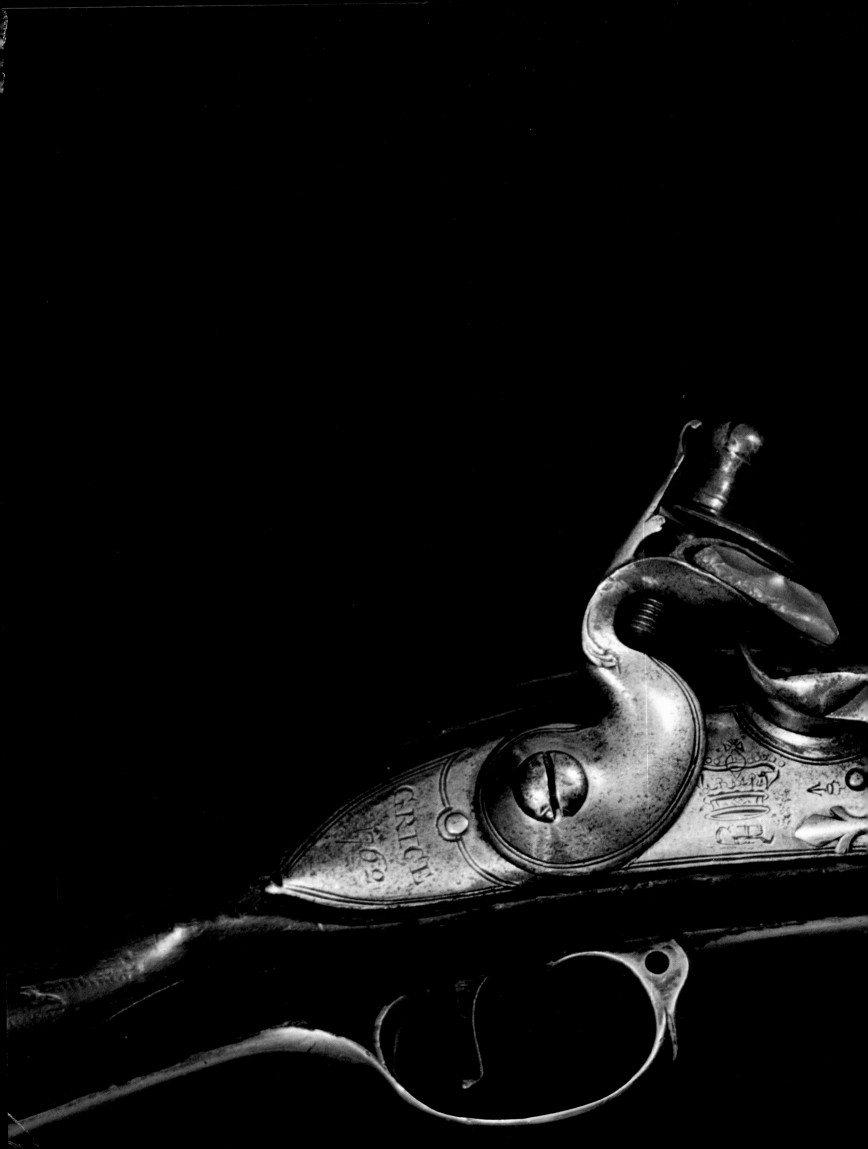

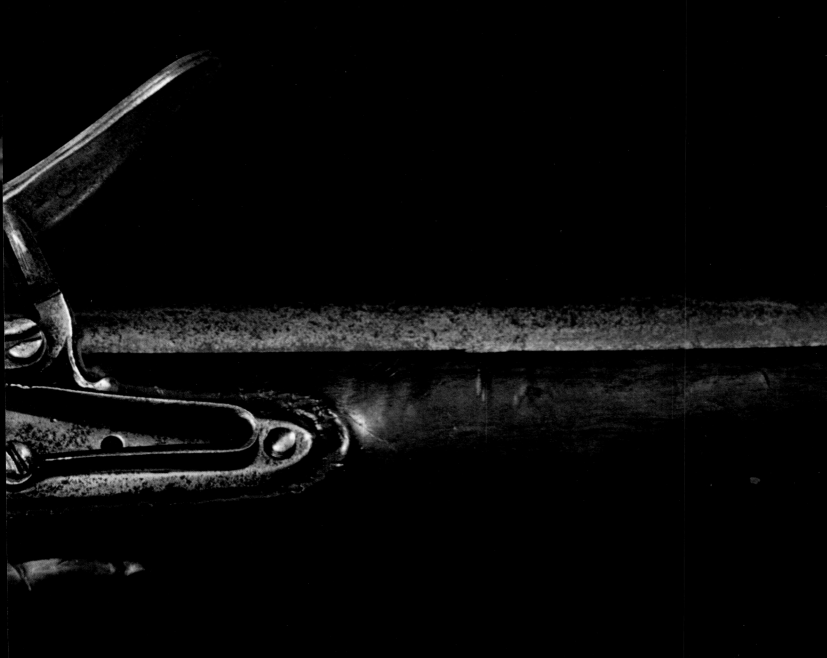

The Pleasure of Guns

the intricate and beautiful work of famous gunsmiths

Joseph G. Rosa & Robin May

OCTOPUS

Octopus Books

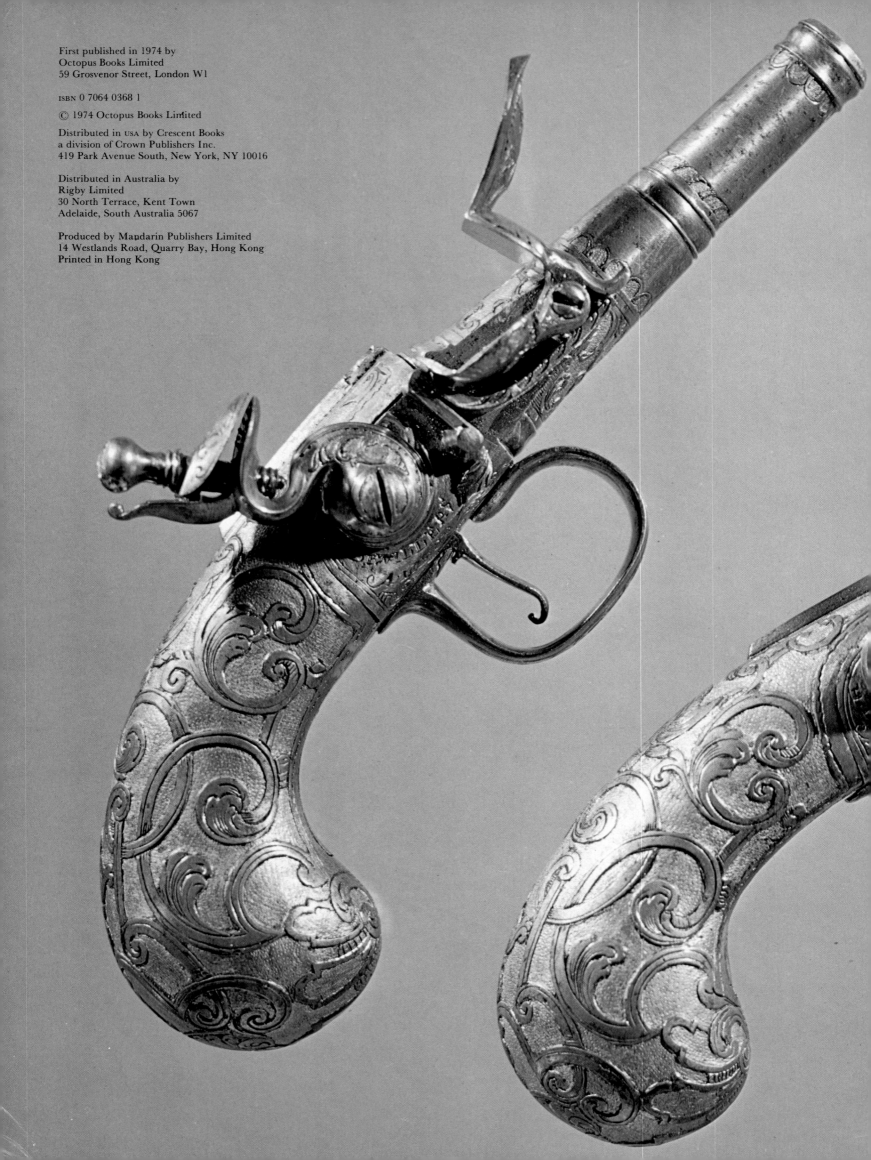

First published in 1974 by
Octopus Books Limited
59 Grosvenor Street, London W1

ISBN 0 7064 0368 1

© 1974 Octopus Books Limited

Distributed in USA by Crescent Books
a division of Crown Publishers Inc.
419 Park Avenue South, New York, NY 10016

Distributed in Australia by
Rigby Limited
30 North Terrace, Kent Town
Adelaide, South Australia 5067

Produced by Mandarin Publishers Limited
14 Westlands Road, Quarry Bay, Hong Kong
Printed in Hong Kong

Contents

Myths,
Matchlocks &
Wheel-locks

Gunpowder reached star status as a war weapon when the unfortunate James II of Scotland was 'dung in two by a piece of misframed gune that brake in the shutting, by which he . . . died hastilie'. This happened in 1460 at the siege of Roxburgh, by which time it had been used in warfare for many years.

Just how long has always been a matter of conjecture, for as with so many inventions and discoveries, nobody (except, apparently, the omniscient authors of the third-rate school textbooks and popular encyclopedias) knows exactly when the crucial moment occurred.

Some believe that it was the Chinese who first mixed saltpetre, charcoal and sulphur and produced gunpowder; others claim that the Arabs, while Europe was enduring the Dark Ages, devised the deadly brew. In Asia, saltpetre had certainly been added to chemical concoctions, but not necessarily to make explosive mixtures. The 'Greek Fire', used by the Byzantines against the hordes of Islam who besieged Constantinople in the seventh century, was a non-explosive but potentially lethal mixture of naptha, sulphur and pitch.

Two names are often put forward for consideration. The first, despite his presence in European schoolbooks, can be quickly dismissed. He was Bertold Schwarz and a statue of him was put up in Freiburg-im-Breisgau to commemorate his invention of gunpowder in 1353. This was so inconveniently late that some supporters have claimed his real invention to have been the cannon. Others have unsportingly denied that he ever existed.

A safer bet is the remarkable Franciscan, Roger Bacon (*c.* 1214–92). A Somerset man who studied at Oxford and in Paris, he was a keen scientist, and his writings got him ten years in prison for dabbling in magic. These works contain a cryptogram which, when rearranged, shows that he knew the secret of gunpowder, even if he did not invent it. He was also sufficiently far-sighted to see the effect it might have on warfare. Although it took many centuries to get first-rate saltpetre, the result was soon evident for the invention transformed the pattern of warfare and thus of the medieval world.

Thirteenth-century Europe, like the rest of the world, fought with weapons that were variations on common themes: the sword, the lance, the battleaxe and the bow. The legendary English longbow, which was actually developed in Wales, was feared all over Europe after the battle of Crécy (1346). Handled by professionals, at 250 yards it produced a hail of arrows, the concentrated effect of which remained unequalled until the American Civil War.

The crossbow, although more powerful and much simpler to use, could only despatch one arrow to the longbow's six to twelve. The very efficient short Turkish bow was vulnerable to damp and suited only to dry climates. Provided the string did not get too wet, therefore, the longbow was the best all-weather weapon.

Before gunpowder made 'all men alike tall', as Thomas Carlyle noted, war – for the top people – was a chivalrous business. It was up to a knight to defend his own or someone else's honour on a strictly man-to-man basis. The large supporting body of infantry providing the backcloth to such valorous deeds was regarded as a necessary evil. Most noblemen had little but contempt for the peasants who made up their armies, and even in the hands of Genoese professionals, the crossbow was considered an ungentlemanly weapon. The sword, however, with its certain destination, was an honourable tool. The admiration shown by Edward III and his nobles for their bowmen was contrary to all the rules. If guns brought true democracy to the battlefields of Europe, it was the bowmen of England at Crécy and Poitiers who began the process.

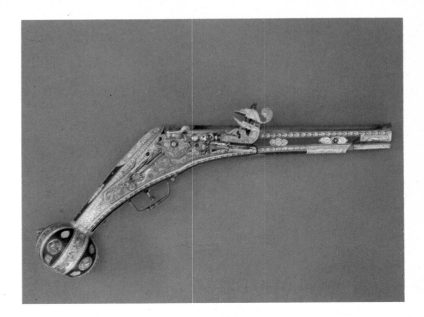

PREVIOUS PAGES *The wheel-lock is said to have been invented either in southern Germany or northern Italy. Their makers paid as much attention to the locks as to the stocks. Note the intricacy of the detail and the design of this ivory and pearl-inlaid specimen. Immediately below the pan can be seen the square spindle (similar to that found in clocks or clockwork toys), on which the key, or winding spanner, was fitted. As the key was turned, a short chain attached to the mainspring caused it to 'wind up'. After the 'dog' (or pyrites holder) was lowered into the pan, the wheel was released, spinning against the pyrites and showering sparks into the pan, thus setting off the powder and charge.*

TOP *This superb wheel-lock pistol was made* c. *1580 in Germany by Wolf Stapler of Nuremburg. Note the fine decoration.*

ABOVE *The siege of a town, from* Chroniques d'Angleterre. *This graphic illustration shows what a devastating effect gunpowder and the 'new fangled' firearms must have had on warfare in the 14th and 15th centuries. It is interesting to note that both the crossbow and the longbow are still being used in conjunction (the former, with its greater penetration, being preferred in Europe). But it is the huge mortar in the centre that commands most attention. This was one of the earliest of large artillery pieces, so named because of its superficial resemblance, as originally devised, to the vessel used by apothecaries.*

The idea of actually hurling a projectile by means of gunpowder may not have been tried out until around 1300, and handguns, which were mini-cannons at first, appeared half a century later. A key date was 1326, for in that year the Council of Florence ordered iron bullets and metal barrels to be made for the defence of the city (a document survives to prove it). In that same year Edward III was given a manuscript by his chaplain, Walter de Milemete, which has a coloured picture of a vaselike gun that fired a dart. A knight is shown lighting the charge and the gun appears to be brass. At last we have proof positive.

Early cannon seem to have been simple barrels or tubes, into which were poured the powder, stones or arrows. After the shot was rammed down, the charge was ignited by means of a touch-hole, into which was thrust a red-hot 'firing iron'.

So the 'devil's invention', as some cursed it, inspired a more sinister approach to the business of killing. Although handguns might have a slow rate of fire, they could pierce armour; and even if individually inaccurate, enough of them aimed at a crowd could cause heavy casualties. By the end of the sixteenth century they had made bows obsolete. War as a knightly sport was finished.

shaped bar, pivoted in the middle. Beneath it was a pan containing powder which filtered through a touch-hole into the barrel, and when the 'serpentine' (as the match-holder was sometimes called) was lowered, the powder was ignited and the gun discharged.

Gunmakers even then appreciated the value of appearance, and made great efforts to outshine their rival craftsmen. Meanwhile, as it developed, the matchlock underwent various changes in different countries. This resulted in baffling references to hackbuts, hakbuchsen, harquebueses, arquebuses, calivers and petronels. Arquebus meant a weapon fired from the shoulder or chest without a rest.

Though the matchlock survived in varying forms until the late nineteenth century (principally in Japan and India), it was superseded in its own days of glory by a weapon with a far more complicated lock. This was the famous, and still much-admired, wheel-lock, which may be compared with a modern cigarette lighter. A wheel or disc of hardened steel with a serrated rim had a spindle protruding from its centre. This was attached to a small chain, which was connected to a very powerful mainspring. When the wheel was turned, or wound by means of a key or crank, pressure was placed on the main-

Once invented, they were steadily improved. Wooden stocks were introduced in the fourteenth century to help cope with the recoil problem and the heat of the metal; and to speed up the means of ignition the matchlock came into being. What would now be called the 'action' or 'lockwork' appeared with the introduction of the 'match' and the device for holding it.

The match was simply a loosely twisted rope, or hemp 'wick', which had been soaked in a solution of saltpetre and spirits of wine. When lit, it burned very slowly like a live, glowing coal. Later, the match-holder was attached to the gun. In this form the holder was an S-

spring by the chain turning on the spindle. It was kept wound by a simple trigger-like device, which, once released, allowed the wheel to spin with great force. A portion of the wheel protruded into the priming pan, and pressed against it by a spring was a small piece of iron pyrite which gave off sparks. At the same time as the wheel was released by the trigger, another part of the lock pushed aside a cover exposing the pan to the sparks from the iron pyrite. These were directed into the powder and ignited the charge. Although the description sounds complicated, the wheel-lock was simple to use and was soon developed very successfully.

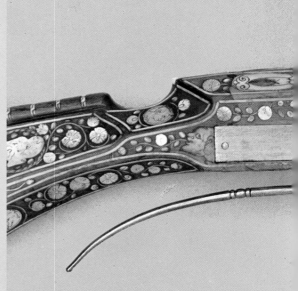

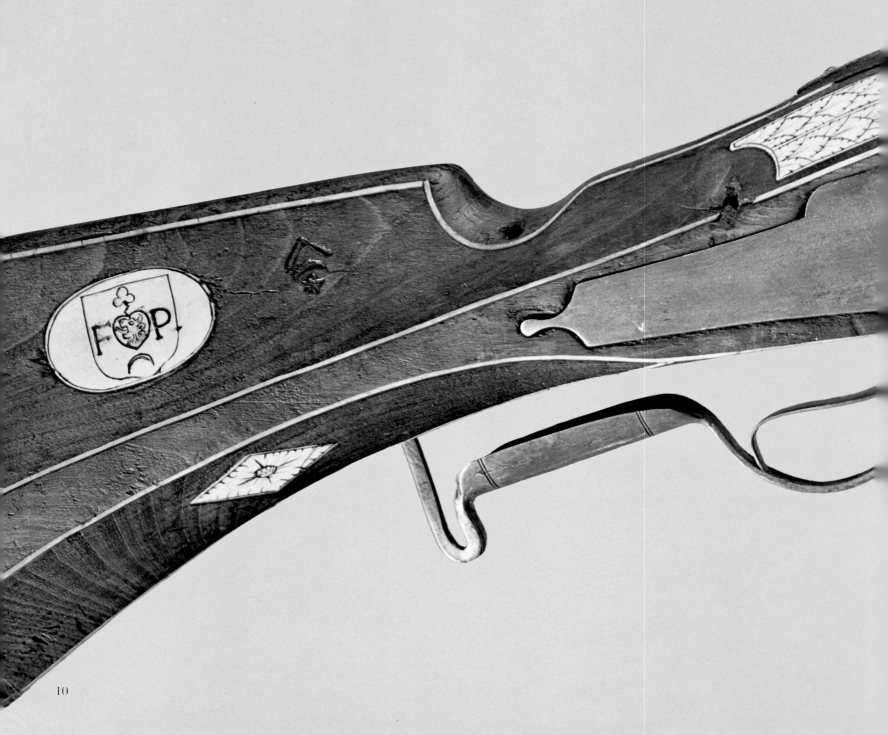

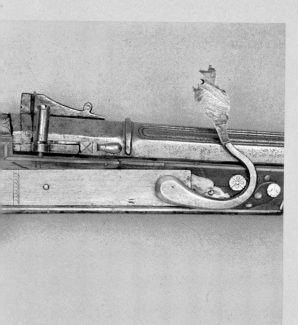

Far left top This plain but efficient-looking matchlock is notable for the finely-chiselled coat of arms of Pope Julius III on the top of the barrel. It was made in Turin.

Far left below The entire barrel and metalwork of this Turin-made matchlock have been etched and then gilt. Unlike some of its contemporaries, the stock on this weapon is quite plain, with the exception of the inlays on the edges, which are finely executed.

Left The Germans were adept in combining beauty with utility, as this matchlock musket, made about 1600, shows. A beautiful specimen with a stock finely inlaid with mother-of-pearl and bone, it is fitted with the improved searlock which appeared toward the end of the 15th century. It was simple and comparatively cheap to make. The long sear lever pivoted vertically inside the lock plate, under pressure from the mainspring. At one end was linked the serpentine (match-holder) and at the other an extension lever, which functioned as a trigger. Tension from the mainspring held the serpentine away from the pan, but pressure on the extension lever forced it downward into the priming powder.

Below Made well after the invention of the wheel-lock, this matchlock musket is dated 1610 and bears the initials F P on the stock. It was probably carried by the private guard of a nobleman. Note that the lock is fitted with a dummy wheel, giving the plain lock-plate the appearance of a wheel-lock, more pleasing to the eye.

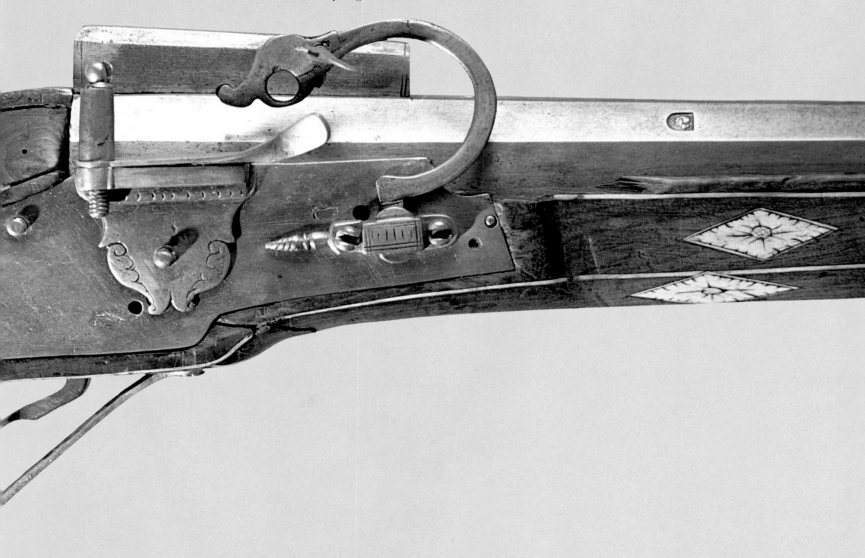

Left This remarkable print depicts bullocks dragging siege guns for an attack in 1568 on the fort at Ranthambhor Rajastan in India, during the reign of the great Mogul emperor, Akbar. Already it can be seen how gunpowder was influencing warfare in the East. A close examination of the fine detail shows a remarkable collection of weapons being used, including matchlocks.

Right Janissaries of Sultan Suleyman the Magnificent advancing to attack a castle on Lake Van, occupied by the Persians, in 1548–9. Note how they carry their matchlocks ready for instant use. Janissaries were the famous militia of the Ottoman Empire and were first raised in the late 14th century as the nucleus of a standing army, being allowed to choose and expected to provide their own weapons. Involved in many palace revolutions, they were massacred in 1826, when they rose in revolt against Mahmud II, and disbanded.

Below An interesting 18th-century Indian revolving matchlock gun discovered by Samuel Colt in London in 1851. It had belonged to Lord William Bentinck, a one-time Governor-General of India. The gun is well made but unmarked. Colt noted that 'the breech, which requires to be moved by the hand, has five chambers, each having a priming pan with a swing cover. The arbor [the pin on which the cylinder revolves] is attached to the barrel, which, at the end adjoining the breech, is enlarged to correspond with the diameter of the revolving chamber, to which it forms a kind of shield'.

Bottom The 17th-century Turkish matchlock shown at the top is a very simple and crude weapon compared with the early 19th century 'Mediterranean' or 'miquelet' lock rifle illustrated on page 24.

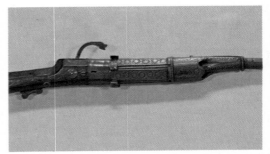

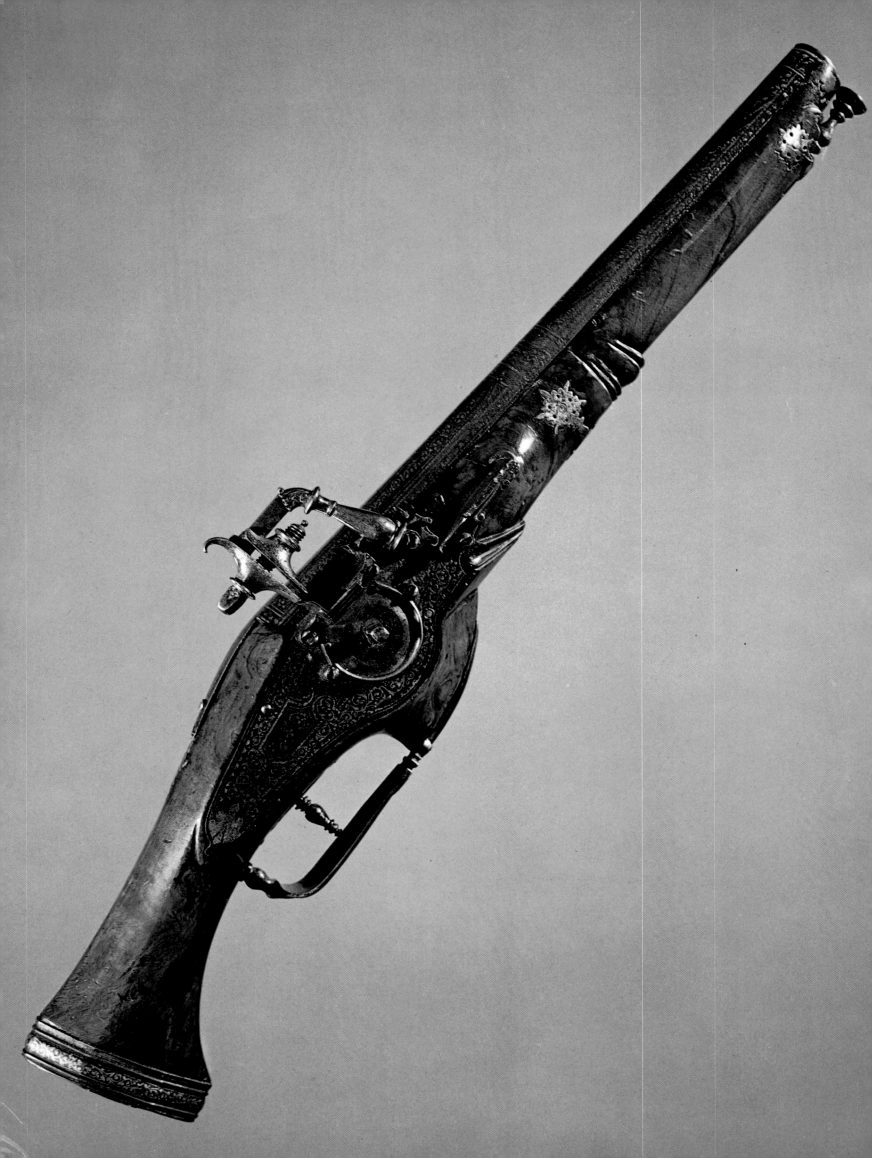

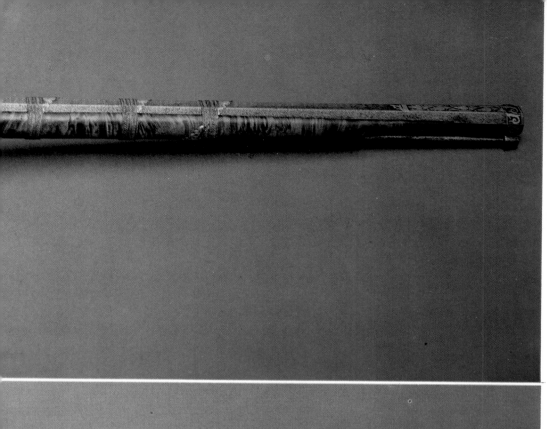

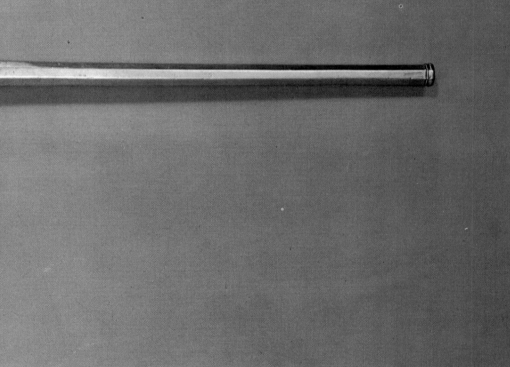

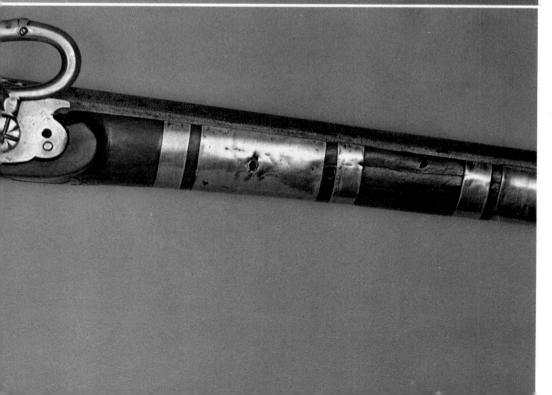

Top A 19th-century Turkish rifle fitted with a Turkish-type miquelet lock. The stock is typical of Turkish longarms of both 18th and 19th centuries, and is decorated in gold, silver and green-stained ivory. The bands securing the barrel are hammered silver, gold inlaid, and the lock is overlaid with gold.

Centre This snaphaunce revolving gun is credited to the London gunmaker, John Dafte, and was made in about 1680. It is .46 calibre six-shot gun, $33\frac{1}{8}$-inch in length, with a $14\frac{3}{8}$-inch barrel and weighs 5lbs 2oz. The cylinder is revolved by hand, either clockwise or counterclockwise. A cylinder locking bar with a pin engages with stops cut into the periphery of the cylinder, close to the front. The pan covers are brass plates which slide in grooves, and are actuated by an arm attached to the hammer. In 1851, Samuel Colt read a paper before the Institute of Civil Engineers in London which led to his being elected an associate member and the recipient of the Telford Medal. Not surprisingly, the subject was the manufacture of fire-arms by machinery, and this gun was among the weapons used to illustrate both his lecture and the published paper.

Bottom Matchlocks, many of them made in Japan, continued to be popular well into the 19th century. This specimen, however, is one of the late non-Oriental versions, of Spanish-American origin. It is dated 1844 and, as can be seen, the brasswork is crudely engraved. The lock is of the simple sear-type, and the butt is a copy of the popular Catalan style.

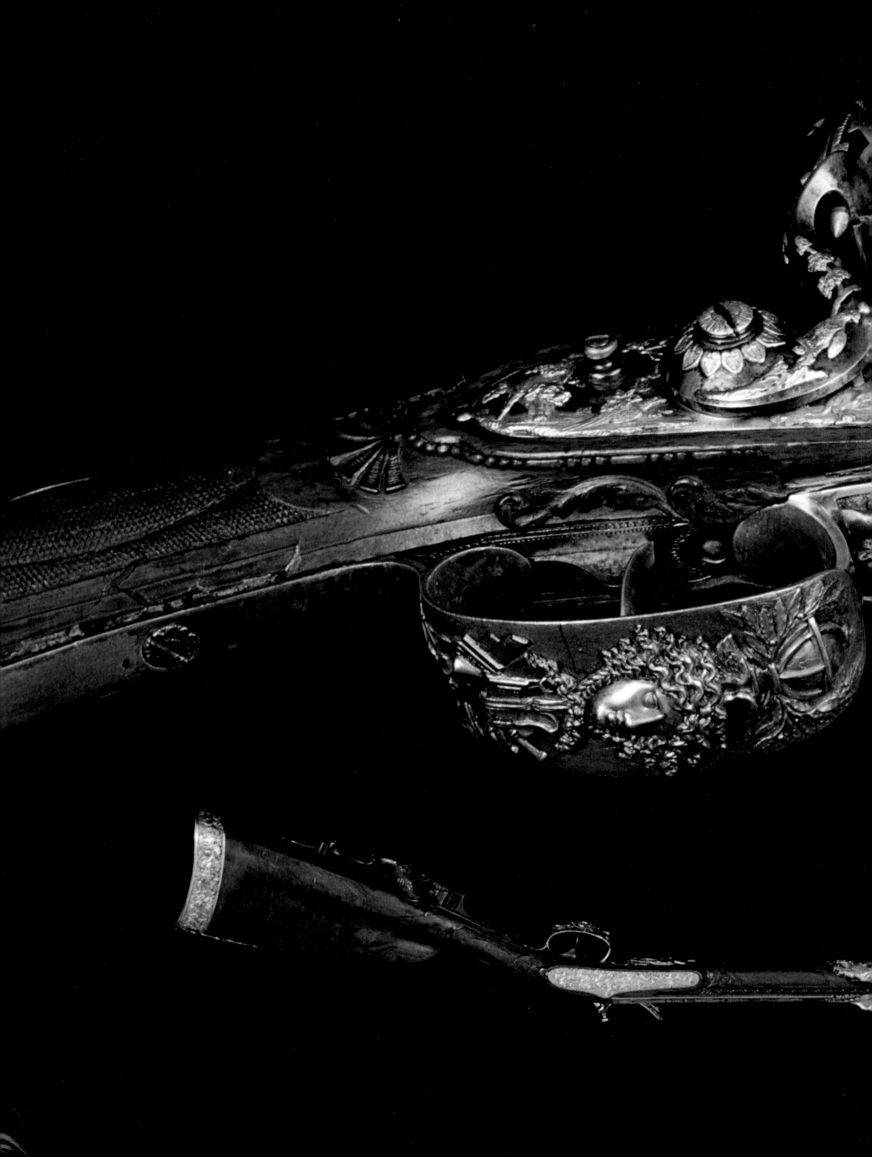

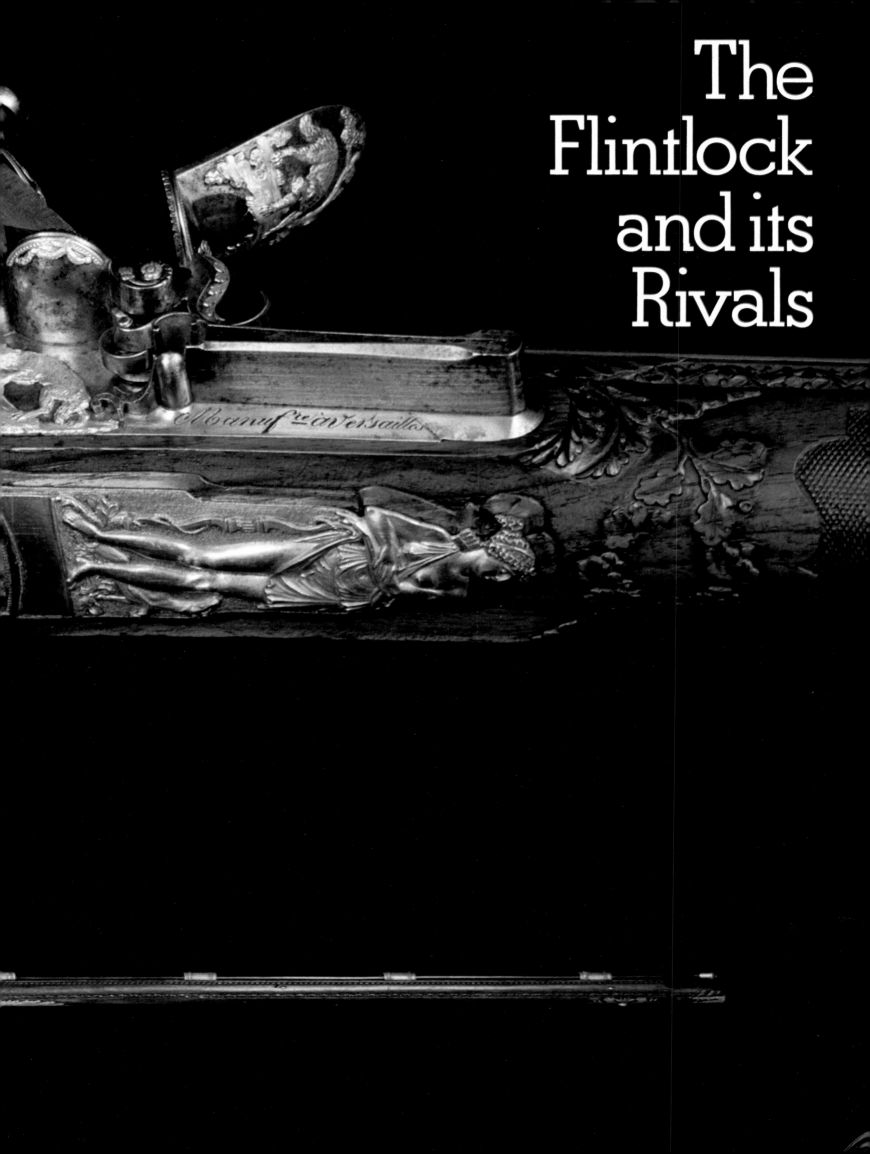

The Flintlock and its Rivals

On 13 September 1759, the thin line of British soldiers stood like carved stone on the Heights of Abraham as the French came on at a run. Not until they were as close as 40 yards did General Wolfe give the order to fire, and the most decisive single volley in history destroyed French Canada.

The Brown Bess flintlock was the weapon that caused the havoc. Always accurate enough at short range, especially when fired by a mass of disciplined troops, on this occasion it surpassed itself. That volley was described by Sir John Fortescue, historian of the British Army, as the most perfect ever fired on a battlefield, and although it took another year to effect the total collapse of French Canada, the issue was never in doubt. It did more than give Britain Canada. Freed from the French menace, her thirteen American colonies were given a breathing space, and sixteen years later won their independence from Britain. It was the proudest moment in the long history of the Brown Bess and indeed of the flintlock.

'Long' is the operative word. The wheel-lock was a mechanical marvel, but it was complicated, and was soon rivalled by other, less difficult forms of 'spark ignition'. Exactly what some of those early developments were remains a mystery. Scholars were vague when writing about guns in the late fifteenth and early sixteenth centuries, and not until the 1540s is there documentary evidence that wheel-locks had given way to other forms of ignition, already common in Italy, Sweden and Holland. Of those we know about, the most important was the snaphaunce, which originated, depending on one's preference, in Scandinavia, Holland or Italy. Its strange name is certainly from the Flemish, and some legends attribute its invention to Dutch thieves and poachers, who had apparently been too easily detected by farmers' dogs when carrying glowing coals on matchlocks. So, the story goes, the cunning poachers invented a lock which dispensed with the usual match and used a striker. This was the origin of the *schnap hähner*, or 'chicken-snatchers' lock! A splendid explanation, but as fictional, alas, as William Tell. The truth may be that the early Dutch lock, when cocked and fired, reminded people of the pecking of a farmyard rooster. Anyway, the *schnapp-hahn* or 'pecking cock' (the flint vice was called a *hahn* or cock, and the steel against which it struck was known as the hen) rapidly became popular; and the name became corrupted as it spread round Europe to snaphaunce or snaphance, a term which has survived.

The snaphaunce was a weapon which had a large-S-shaped cock containing a flint. The pan containing the priming powder was fitted with a sliding cover activated, when fired, by the cock. The steel against which the flint struck to produce sparks was controlled by a spring, which allowed it to be positioned directly above the pan, or tipped forward out of the way. This latter action produced a safety factor, for unless the steel was in position any accidental tripping of the hammer or cock would not discharge the weapon.

The Dutch were great traders and the 'pecking roosters' reached as far north as Scandinavia (if indeed they did not start there) and as far south as Africa. They were later copied there and, amazingly, 'early' snaphaunces were still being made in Morocco in the 1880s.

One refinement of the snaphaunce was the miquelet, a superior mechanism which was very popular in Spain and Italy. The key factor with this gun was the combination of the steel and the pan. When the cock fell and its flint struck the steel (now L-shaped), which was hinged and held in place by a spring, it knocked it forward, at the same time exposing the pan to the sparks.

A difference between the fashionable locks of the time and the miquelet lock was the presence of the mainspring on the outside of the lock plate—an innovation that proved popular in the Middle East, where, until recently, it was still being used.

The French produced the first true 'flintlock', and the name of the inventor is actually known. He had frog-like eyes, a peasant's face and the soul of a poet; he was a sculptor, painter and maker of musical instruments. His name was Marin le Bourgeoys and he was one of a family of great gunsmiths (see pages 66–7).

This remarkable man from Normandy was also a manufacturer of crossbows and a gunsmith. So talented and versatile was he that even the authorities took notice. In 1608 he was appointed as artist-cum-

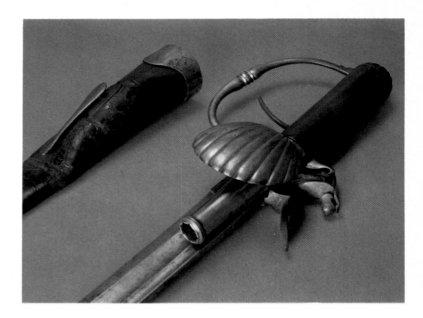

TOP *Sword pistols are rare collector's items. This flintlock sword pistol has an iron barrel, and the trigger is in the centre of the handle. A noteworthy feature is the shell-like cover, which serves as a form of protection to both the pistol and the hand.*

ABOVE *A single shattering volley from British Brown Bess muskets prepared the way for victory against the French on the Heights of Abraham in 1759, and led eventually to the British occupation of Canada. This engraving compresses a sequence of events into a single moment from the landing below the cliffs to the battle on the plain above.*

PREVIOUS PAGES *This superb flintlock rifle is the work of Nicolas Noël Boutet, gunmaker to Napoleon, who had his factory at Versailles. Its workmanship and ornamentation are breathtaking. Particularly fascinating is the gold-encrusted decoration on the lock-plate, cock and pan.*

inventor to the court of King Henry IV and continued in his post under Louis XIII for whom he made the first flintlock shortly after his accession.

The le Bourgeoys or French flintlock, which was widely copied, combined the snaphaunce with the miquelet. From the latter came the combined steel and pan cover (now called the frizzen), from the former was developed the internal mainspring which rested on a tumbler. But le Bourgeoys' most important contribution was the redesigning of the sear, that part of the action which bears upon the hammer notches or 'bents' that provide the half-cock and full-cock positions. In earlier weapons this had moved laterally or sideways, but now it had a vertical movement. The improvement in safety and the strength of the lock were quickly realized, and the fame of the invention spread. By the mid-1630s it was known all over Europe.

Each country developed its own version of the flintlock. It altered the whole concept of military hand weapons. With only minor improvements, the flintlock remained the standard ignition for 200 years.

Enthusiasts quickly adapted the new lock to fowling pieces and sporting guns. Pocket pistols became safer and, with the flintlock,

culminated in the famous Charleville arms, which were copied by American gunsmiths. Later, the United States Government arms also closely followed French models. But Britain produced the most famous musket of all, the Brown Bess.

For more than a century this smoothbore weapon was the standard infantry arm of the British soldier. How it got its name is a matter for dispute. Brown merely referred to the practice of browning the barrels to prevent rust. 'Bess' is either from the German *buchse*, meaning gun, or (more probably) someone's pet name. Earlier arms had been given black-painted stocks, but the Bess was fitted with fine brown walnut stocks.

Its length of service was due to its remarkable durability, simplicity of action and comparative reliability. As a smoothbore, its accuracy was questionable, but, except in forest and woodland warfare, this did not matter tactically. Several thousand Besses all fired into enemy ranks at 50–200 yards provided real fire power.

Washington's men faced the Brown Bess, and so did the French in the Peninsula and at Waterloo, where the British squares decimated the French cavalry. Even when it was obsolete, the British sold

the true duelling pistol appeared. But the main benefit was to the army. By 1700, British military arms were no longer second-class in design or status, and were now standardized and produced in quantity. And all over Europe, particularly in France and Germany, guns poured from national armouries at an ever-increasing rate.

By 1715, the British Government had reorganized the Ordnance system of manufacture so that, as far as possible, all arms parts were made in Britain. But it did not always work in wartime. Parts were made in London and Birmingham and assembled, 'lock, stock and barrel' in either city, causing inevitable delays. So, as late as the nineteenth century, arms were still being purchased from Europe.

The flintlock musket dominated the battlefields of Europe and America from the early 1700s to the 1820s. In France, modifications

thousands to Latin America, which meant that in the war against Mexico in 1846–47 the Americans once again found themselves facing the musket of the War of Independence and the War of 1812.

Rivalling the Brown Bess in the War of Independence was the legendary Kentucky rifle, a small-calibred but highly accurate weapon derived from the earlier German Jaeger rifles.

By now the flintlock was a very formidable weapon. Provided it got proper care and attention, that its flints were replaced regularly, and its powder kept dry, it was a good, dependable companion. Refinements were innumerable and by the early nineteenth century it was at its peak as both a smoothbore and a rifled musket. Yet the ultimate in flintlocks proved to be ahead of its time and failed to receive the attention it deserved. This was the Ferguson breechloading rifle.

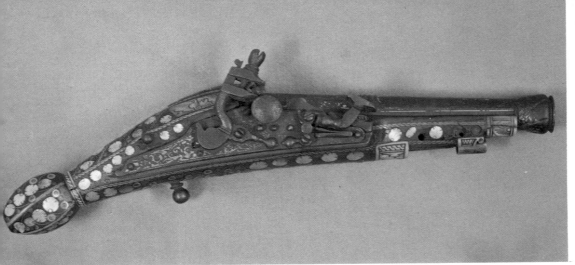

Top left This fine English snaphaunce pistol (early 17th century) shows the strong influence of European master gunmakers of the period. The familiar wheel-lock shape is retained, but the improved lock already gives a foretaste of things to come. The stock is inlaid with horn and mother-of-pearl.

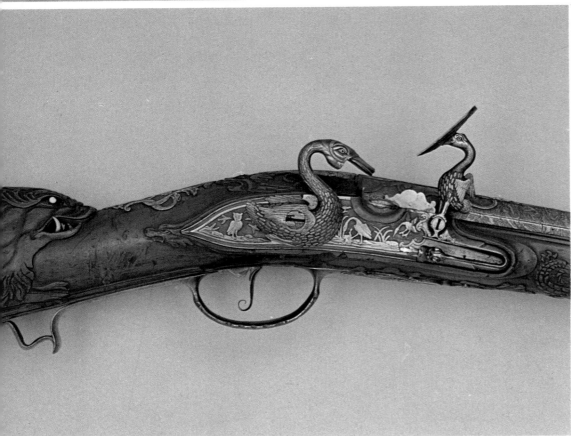

Centre left The stock of this gun, made *c.* 1685, is a woodcarver's delight. The unusual snaphaunce lock is in the shape of a swan, the flint being held in its beak; and another smaller swan grasps the steel. The damascus barrel was fashioned by turning red hot strips of metal on a mandrel, which were hammered together, flattened, and filed to shape. The barrel is in the Turkish style, and the lock and the other iron work are all encrusted with silver and decorated with grotesque animals and foliage. Although the butt is fluted the weapon shows German influence.

Bottom left The Spaniards were skilled makers of sporting guns. This specimen is the work of Mathias Quero of Malaga and is dated 1742. The plate of this miquelet lock is longer than usual.

Top right A fine pair of 17th-century brass scroll-butted snaphaunce pistols from Scotland. The butt shape varied considerably, and later arms had what was called a 'ram's horn' because of the shape of the horn-like prongs placed at either end of the butt, which tended to turn inwards. The ram's horn form was still found in the following century, but the majority of Scottish pistols of the 18th and 19th centuries were made entirely of steel.

Bottom right A handsome pair of snaphaunce pistols with barrels by Lazzarino Cominazzo, made in Brescia at the end of the 17th century. The barrels are octagonal at the breech and incised with longitudinal lines on the upper plane. The locks, chiselled in relief with monsters and floral scrolls, are complemented by similar work in the stocks. Note the long belt hook on the left side of the upper pistol. The Cominazzo family were the most celebrated barrelsmiths in the area, and the founder of the firm, also Lazzarino, had worked for Vincenzo Gonzaga, Duke of Mantua, in 1593.

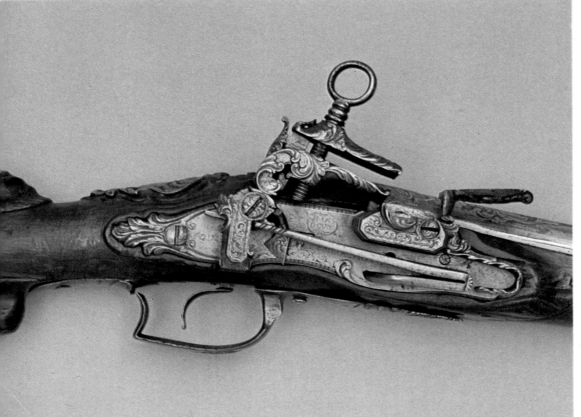

Loading Procedures for Flintlock and Cap and Ball Pistols

We have described the operation of the matchlock, the wheel-lock, the flintlock and the percussion lock, but not the loading procedure. Basically, this was common to all four. First, a measured charge of powder was poured down the barrel, and a ball rammed down on top. The pan was then primed with fine powder, which, when ignited by the glowing match, or sparks from the steel and flint (in the case of the percussion lock, the cap was struck by the hammer), despatched a flame into the touch hole. This set off the charge and sped the ball on its way.

Left The British 'Brown Bess' was perhaps the most famous musket ever produced. Used for over 200 years, even as late as the 1840s, it was one of the principal weapons in the army of the Mexican dictator, Santa Anna. This specimen by Grice is dated 1762, and is one of the now rare 46-in barrelled versions (many of them were cut back to 42in). The lockplate bears the maker's name and also the royal cypher and G R, which was stamped on weapons issued to the British Army. The plate also shows the broad arrow denoting Board of Ordnance inspection.

Below This exceptional example of a double-barrelled flintlock rifle was made *c.* 1805 by the great Boutet at Versailles. The barrels are placed over-and-under, and each has a separate pan served by one lock. The barrels turn over making it an interesting combination weapon, for one barrel is

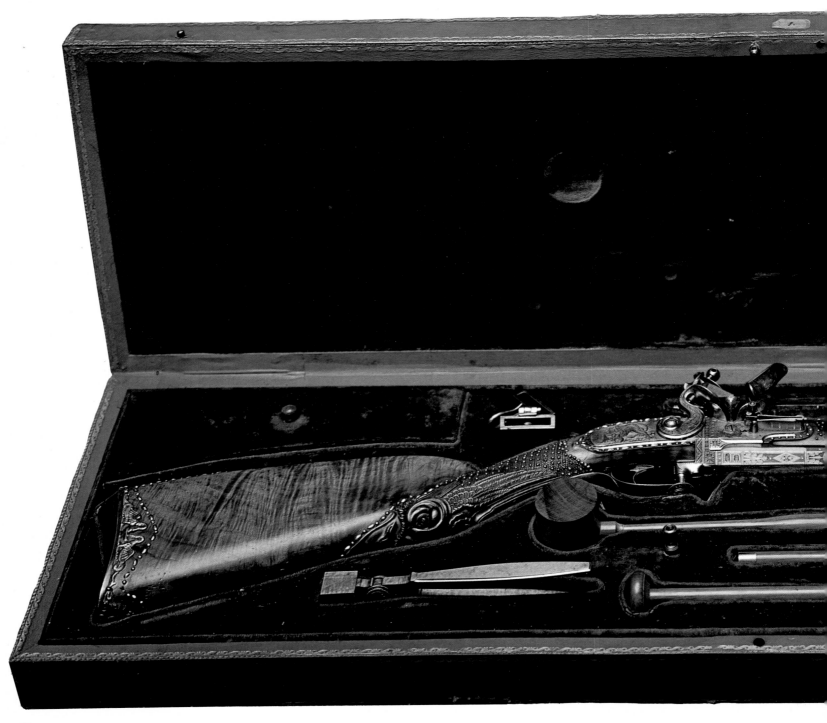

rifled with twelve grooves, while the other is smooth bored. The muzzle and breech are in gilt, and the stock inlaid with fine silver studs. This weapon is thought to have been presented to the Czar Nicholas I of Russia (1825–55).

Right top This magnificent all-brass Scottish snaphaunce gun is handsomely ornamented, and is the work of James Low of Dundee. Dated 1624, there is only one other of this type known to be in existence.

Right below A fine example of the English flintlock sporting rifle of the 1740s fitted with a Russian barrel. The lock is signed by Joseph Griffin. The fine walnut stock with its brass mounts, bears the arms of John, 4th Lord Carmichael and 3rd Earl of Hyndford, a Scottish diplomat, who was sent to Moscow during the 1740s to help negotiate the peace of Aix-la-Chapelle, which ended the war of the Austrian succession.

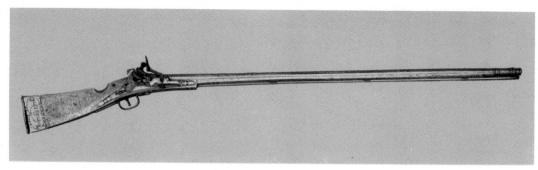

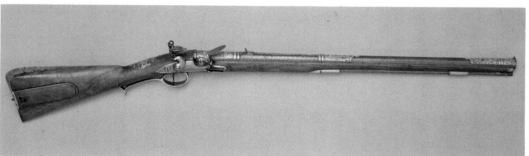

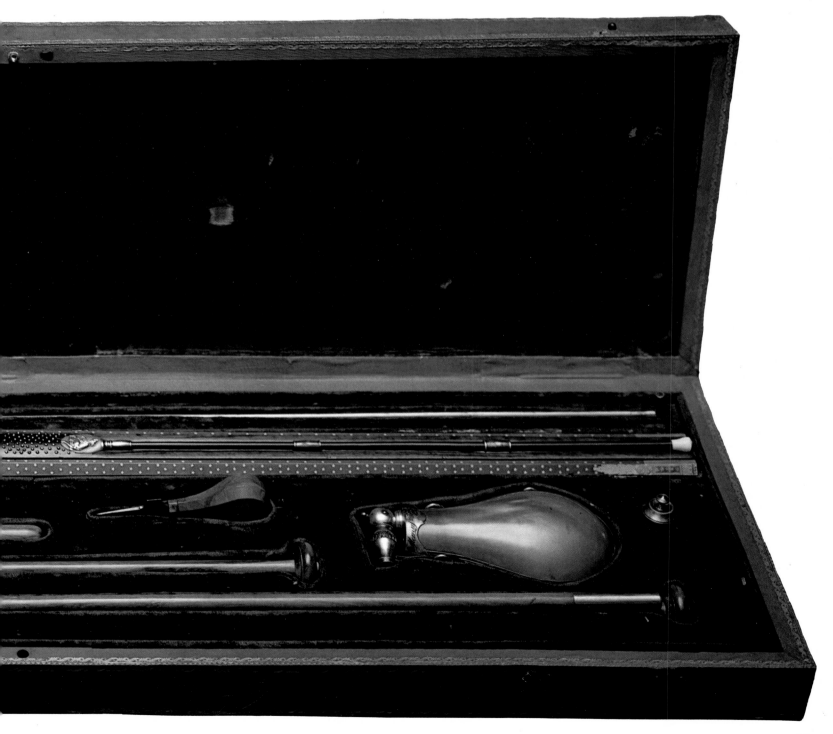

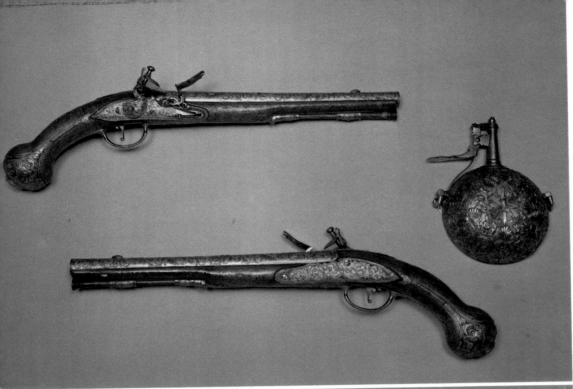

Top left A fine pair of Russian pistols, made in 1752, complete with powder flask. The ornamentation on both pistols and flask, particularly the chiselling of the steel, is of the highest quality. The first small-arms factory in Russia had been established by Peter the Great some 50 years previously. Early Russian guns had an Oriental appearance, but European gunmakers who settled in Russia introduced European taste.

Centre left Henry Hadley, the London gunmaker, made this fine pair of silver mounted flintlock holster pistols in the 1750s, for presentation to the 3rd Duke of Marlborough. They have gold inlaid barrels and fine foliate work on the stocks. This was achieved by the time-consuming process of inserting silver wire.

Bottom left A fine pair of Beretta flintlock holster pistols of about 1700, with steel mounts and original steel-tipped ramrods. The Beretta gunmaking family is still in business at Gandone, Brescia, in Northern Italy.

Right The outer pair of these pistols are brass butted and barrelled and are typical of the early 18th century; they are by Louis Barbar, *c.* 1700. The centre pair, *c.* 1750, by James Barbar, are over-and-under barrelled weapons. Each barrel has its own lock, but some versions were made so that the barrels turned and were discharged by one lock.

Some Notes on Duelling

Duelling was either an honourable activity or just plain lunacy, according to your point of view. Mark Antony and Octavius Caesar were classic examples of the two attitudes. Antony, the man of action, challenged the cold, sensible Octavius to personal combat instead of war. He would have none of it. The custom of personal combat goes back to earliest times. Sometimes, as with the unfortunate gladiators of ancient Rome, it was enforced. Through the centuries punishment for duelling has often been severe, but honour must out (if you believe the Hotspurs of this world rather than the Falstaffs), so that men have continued to fight, sometimes for the most trivial reasons. Until the eighteenth century, swords were the most popular means of settling debts of honour, but the pistol gradually replaced the blade. In fact, even in the days of wheel-locks, men fought with pistols. But in the eighteenth century a new breed of pistols began to appear, made specially for the duellist, and with refinements that set them apart from conventional arms. Special sights and 'set' triggers were used, the latter being operated by a spring. One touch of the trigger and the spring did the rest, allowing the shooter to keep a steady aim.

The Duke of Wellington, who once fought a duel himself (see page 38) was so worried by the loss of many of his officers that duelling was banned in the British Army, and in civil law it was a punishable offence. This did not stop it being fashionable for officers and

gentlemen. The French were even keener, while Prussians, for whom duelling was almost a way of life, publicized their exploits by acquiring duelling scars. Strict duelling codes existed, one being drawn up by the gentlemen-delegates of Tipperary, Galway, Sligo, Mayo and Roscommon and settled at Clonmel Summer Assizes in 1777. It was generally followed in Britain and on the Continent, with a few changes, and most of the rules were also adopted in the United States. When fighting a duel, strict attention was paid to procedure. Great care was taken by the seconds to obey rules of etiquette, and even the combatants usually behaved in a gentlemanly way.

By the mid-nineteenth century, duels were becoming increasingly rare in Europe. But in the United States they were replaced by a far more dangerous and, in some quarters, perfectly acceptable means of settling scores – the gunfight. But this is another story. The Code of the West had little to do with the noble (or ignoble) art of duelling.

Left A cased pair of English duelling pistols, made in the 1780s. Probably they were originally fully stocked to the muzzle, but later shortened to conform with the pistols then in fashion. The plain, green baize-lined box is complete with compartments for spare flints, patch cutters, bullet mould, powder flask and cleaning rod/rammer. Many of these weapons were fitted with set triggers which enabled the shooter to exert just enough pressure to discharge the arm without disturbing his aim.

Opposite This fine Heylin flintlock holster pistol was made *c.* 1770, and typifies the high-quality firearms of its day. Note that the silver butt cap (a floral decoration instead of the usual grotesque mask), trigger guard and side plates are ornately engraved. Even the piping beneath the stock to hold the ramrod is finely worked.

Below These two fine pairs of 'Queen Anne' cannon-barrelled flintlock pistols show all the grace of the mid-18th century. A special device fitting over the barrel turned it off so that the pistol could be loaded at the breech without the use of a rammer. The two pistols at the top are by Heylin of London, and the others by T. Richards of London. One pair has the grotesque mask and the other the lion and rampart, similar devices being found on watches as late as the 19th century.

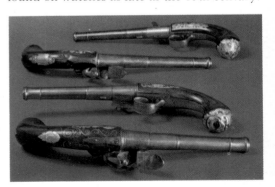

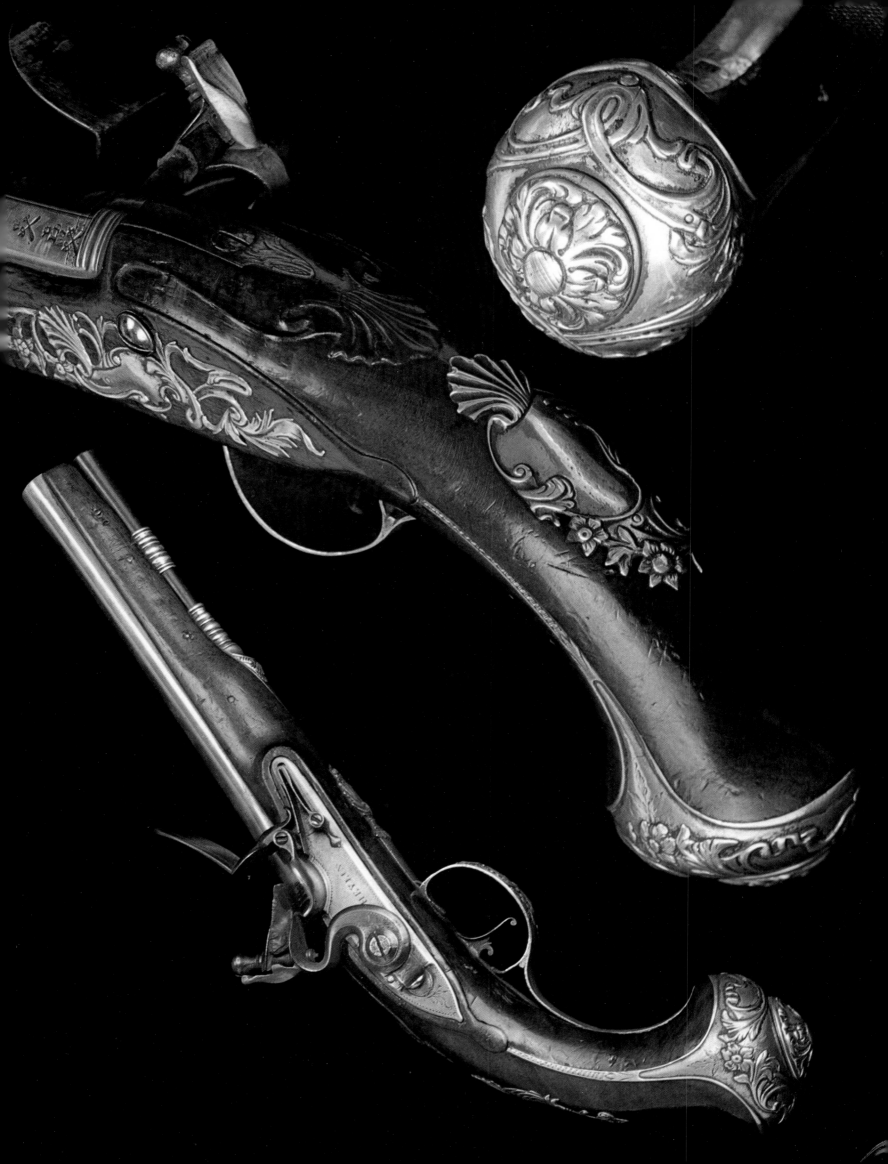

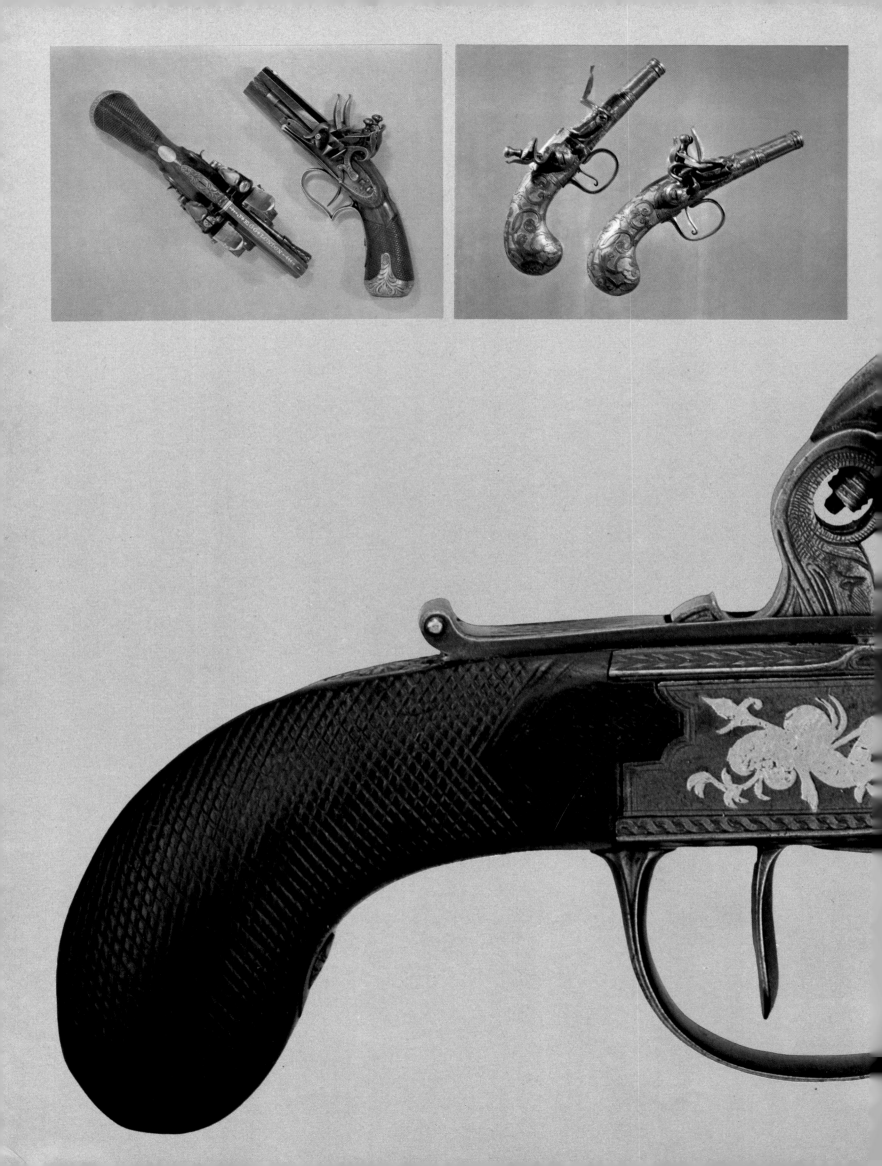

Far left These pocket pistols are hall-marked for 1823–4 and are typical of Joseph Egg's later weapons. Even by the firm's own high standards, the workmanship and attention to detail are remarkable.

Left These all-steel cannon-barrelled pistols of about 1740 are by Devillers of Liège. Their decoration is scroll engraved against a gilt ground. The headquarters of the Belgian gunmaking trade was—and still is—at Liège, one of the most important centres of the craft in Europe.

Below This pocket pistol by Durs Egg was made *c.* 1790 for the Prince of Wales. It is a box-lock (i.e. the flintlock mechanism is confined inside the pistol, rather than on the outside), and, unlike many similar pocket weapons of the time, is also equipped with a rammer. Of particular interest is the solution of the safety problem. When the hammer is placed at half-cock, with the pan cover down, the small pin immediately in front of the hammer base is pushed forward into a small hole in the cover, locking it from premature discharge.

Right A variety of box-lock pistols were produced in the early 19th century. These two examples are particularly interesting because they show the increasing use of steel instead of brass for frames. The brass-bodied version is by Henry Nock; both pistols are nicely rounded.

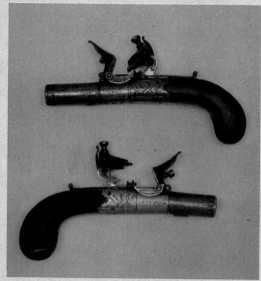

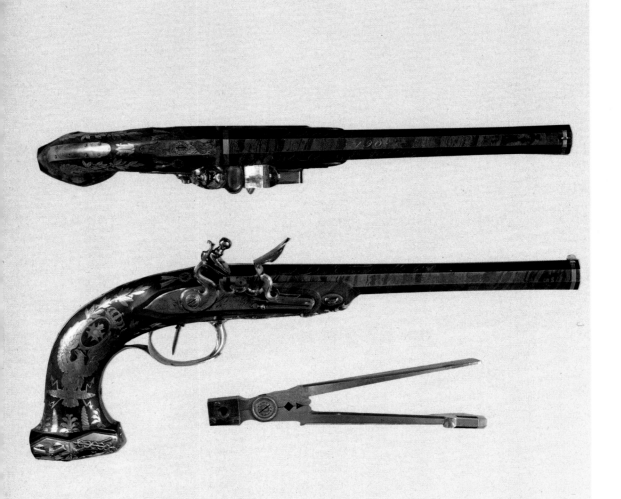

Left Boutet made this fine pair of flintlock pistols at Versailles *c.* 1810. They are typical of his work, both in form and decoration.
Below A superb pair of Boutet pistols, dating from the early 19th century. The silver in the stocks and the gold in the barrels are of a style associated with Boutet and copied by other French gunmakers of this period. Unlike most octagonal barrels, these are swamped. The stock or handle is set at a much sharper angle than the rakish stock of earlier periods.
Right A superb pair of French-export flintlock holster pistols. The barrels are chiselled and gilt, and the finely chiselled locks are also gilt. Gold wire has been used as additional decoration for the stocks, and the lavish effect is completed by jewel-encrusted butt caps. They were made by Claude Bizouard of Marseilles in 1857 and presented to Emperor Franz Joseph I.

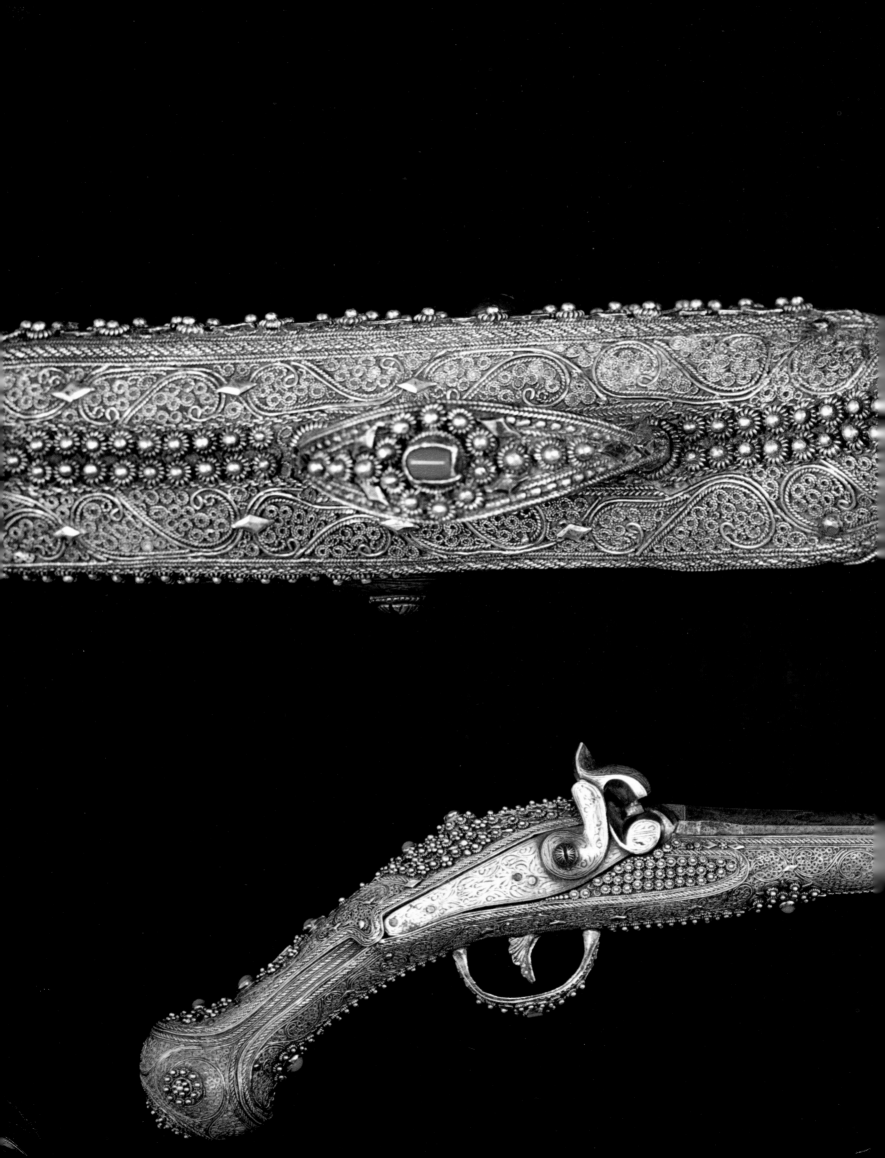

The Percussion Lock

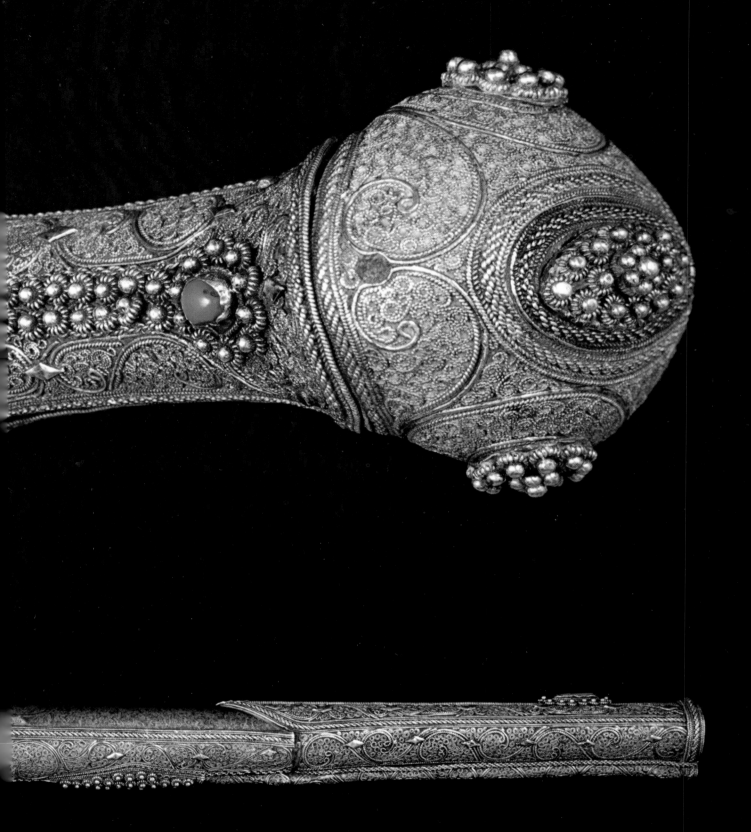

Every French schoolboy knows that the battle of Austerlitz was fought in 1805, and his British counterpart is just as aware that the battle of Trafalgar occurred in the same year. But few children or, for that matter, adults know the other epoch-making events of that year or the name of the obscure sporting parson who made history in terms of the development of the gun.

He was the Reverend Alexander John Forsyth, who had the cure of souls at Belhevie in Aberdeenshire. A keen amateur chemist and mechanic, he was also a mighty hunter, and it was this passion which inspired his revolutionary discovery. Like many of his contemporaries who used flintlocks, he was exasperated when the game he was pursuing saw the flash of powder in the pan before his weapon was discharged, and promptly took evasive action. True, the timelag was only momentary, but it was enough to give the bird a good deal more than sporting chance of escape.

Forsyth, who was born in 1769, was well aware that experiments were in progress to improve gun locks and the priming, but he decided to conduct some of his own.

From his own experiments, and from meeting other enthusiasts, he

was familiar with the known forms of explosives, particularly the various fulminates. In simple terms, these are salts produced by dissolving metals in acids. Once struck, they explode violently, and, as Forsyth knew, care was needed not only in their manufacture but also in handling them. They had been known since at least the seventeenth century, when gold, silver, and potassium chlorate had been produced as fulminates.

In Britain, Edward Howard had devoted time to experimenting with fulminates of mercury, yet he and his predecessors apparently had not thought seriously of employing such devices to set off a charge, least of all in a gun lock. Forsyth, however, thought it could be done and set about doing it.

His experiments, designed to control fulminate of mercury by reducing the amounts to safe, workable proportions, were long and sometimes dangerous, but in 1805 they were successful. By means of a pivoted magazine containing deposits of fulminate of mercury, he was able to seal off any exits for the flame, which was now channelled directly to the bore of the gun.

When it was struck by the hammer, the flame now flashed straight

ABOVE *On 21 March 1829, the Duke of Wellington and the Earl of Winchelsea exchanged shots on Battersea Common. Wags referred to the scene as the 'Battersea Shooting Ground, Grand Pigeon Match'. The duel took place less than a year after Lord Lansdowne's Act made it a hanging offence to 'shoot at another man with intent to kill, disfigure, maim or do him grievous bodily harm.' In his younger days the 'Iron Duke' had banned duelling in the army as likely to take too heavy a toll of officers' lives! In civil law it was a punishable offence. For the record, both eminent pistoleers deliberately missed each other on this occasion.*

PREVIOUS PAGES *Turkish gunmakers were renowned for the decorative qualities of their arms. This splendid specimen, with its watered steel barrel, silver filigree with applied coral decoration, was made in the middle of the 19th century. The back-action lock shows European influence and is typical of weapons manufactured in the 1840s and 1850s.*

to the powder and the weapon was discharged—which must have come as a shock to the birds of Aberdeenshire.

Convinced of his new weapon's potential, he went to London and visited Lord Moira, Master of the Ordnance, to show him his invention. Moira was suitably impressed, but realized that more work was required. So he persuaded the Scottish minister to stay in London, and even offered him employment and facilities at the Tower of London.

Forsyth set to work eagerly, but despite further experiments, the new gun proved disappointing on trial. Lord Moira, meanwhile, had been replaced by the unimaginative Lord Chatham who was not impressed, and banished the inventor and his 'rubbish' from the Tower.

Undismayed, Forsyth continued his work, but saw that he would need capital to continue. Aided by no less a friend than James Watt of steam-engine fame, he applied for and, on 11 April 1807, was granted a patent covering all forms of fulminate and the methods to be employed for priming firearms.

Forsyth's early gun locks, which used the pivoted magazines (there were also some with sliding mechanisms) were quickly dubbed 'scent bottles' because of a resemblance to the perfume bottles then in fashion. They proved very popular with well-to-do sportsmen. But problems of manufacture, expense (this was as much as for a good flintlock) plus the corrosive quality of the fulminates, severely restricted the sales and appeal of the weapons.

Forsyth continued experimenting and became very famous. It is said that at one point Napoleon offered him £20,000 for the secret of his discovery, but patriotically he refused. The year 1843 saw him at last rewarded with a pension, but, ironically, on the day of the first instalment he was found dead in his chair.

Other inventors were also working on clever and dangerous schemes. Among the most interesting ignitions produced in this period were patch primers—fulminate placed between pieces of paper and stuck to the face of the hammer. The hammer struck against a hollow tube exploding the sandwiched fulminate, the flame was directed to the powder and the gun was discharged.

Another equally ingenious device was the 'pill lock', a method by which fulminate, mixed with gum arabic and rolled into little pellets, was placed inside touch-holes and struck by a sharp-pointed hammer.

Then came the 'tube lock'. In this version a metal tube filled with fulminate was inserted in a touch-hole, the top end of which rested on an anvil. The hammer struck this and the flame was sent into the bore. It was not unknown, however, for the flame to flash both ways, sometimes causing terrible facial injury. Alternatively, the force of the explosion might be so great as to blow the whole tube out!

Experiments continued, and although various forms of pill and tube lock were known until the 1850s, the most practical and efficient invention finally proved to be the percussion cap, paving the way towards the modern metallic cartridge.

Credit for this invention is disputed, but many claim that it was an English artist named Joshua Shaw who first introduced a practical 'cap' to replace the previous systems. By mixing the various materials into paste, and placing tiny amounts in minute steel cups or cylinders, it was found that, when placed on the hollow tube or 'nipple' of a firearm, there was enough force to ignite the charge when detonated by the hammer.

Within twenty years, the percussion cap had proved to be the most popular and practical form of ignition. Giant strides were made in its improvement, and the early steel cups or tubes gave way to cups made from very thin sheets of copper. The fulminate of mercury or potassium chlorate, covered by a sheet of tinfoil and sealed with shellac, became the standard ingredient. The system was now much simpler.

At the breech of the gun was screwed the tube or nipple, through the centre of which was drilled a hole leading directly to the powder charge. The cap was placed over the face of the nipple and, when struck by the hammer, it exploded, the flame setting off the charge. Whereas the flintlock had been subject to misfires from poor flints or from damp, the percussion lock proved its reliability under most conditions, and flintlock weapons very gradually disappeared from use.

As with most forms of firearms, it was the sportsmen who first popularized the percussion lock, and the military who followed suit. On the Continent, the percussion lock was quickly adopted by various armies, but Britain was curiously slow at accepting the new system. Nevertheless, the civilian arms trade was soon booming.

Among the most significant trends stemming from the percussion lock was a massive increase in the production of single- and multi-shot pistols. Whereas the flintlock pistol had mainly been designed to be carried in saddle holsters (so that only in the early years of the nineteenth century had pocket or coat pistols been made in any

great number) the invention of the percussion lock inspired the more general use of smaller arms. This was particularly true in the United States where a pistol was as much a part of a man's dress as his trousers or boots.

Perhaps the most famous of all pocket pistols were those made by the Philadelphia gunsmith, Henry Deringer Jr. For years he had been an arms contractor for the U.S. Government, making both military and Indian guns, but after 1825, when he switched to the percussion lock, he concentrated on single-shot pistols. His early arms were long-barrelled weapons, best suited to the belt, but when customers began asking him to cut down the length of the barrels, he experimented with weapons which, although much smaller than his standard arms, retained the large calibres. Tests proved that, despite their size, they were easily handled, and deadly accurate at short ranges.

The response was immediate and Deringer's name became a household word. Scores of his new pocket pistols were ordered and the design became so popular that it was widely copied. Measuring less than 6 inches in length, and with calibres from .36 to .45 (.41 being the most favoured), the 'Deringer', in its way, became as famous as Colt's revolver.

A pair of pistols, made c.1815, by the Rev. Alexander Forsyth's company, complete with powder flask, bullet mould and other accessories. Included in this cased set is an ivory priming flask for detonating powder, with which to fill the magazine. Forsyth's early 'detonating' locks inspired many rivals, and later improvements culminated in the true percussion lock.

Use of the deadly little weapon was not confined to gamblers, gunmen or other violent characters, for even highly respected citizens made a point of carrying these pistols for protection, or for settling personal disputes over politics, women and cards. It was a Deringer which killed Abraham Lincoln, on 14 April 1865, at Ford's Theatre, Washington, only days after the Civil War had ended, the assassin being a crazed actor, John Wilkes Booth. Incidentally, a report of the tragedy established the odd spelling of the name, for a newspaper apparently spelt the murder weapon with two 'r's'. Henceforth, the lethal little pistol became known as a 'Derringer'.

Among the many copies of the basic Derringer were the Remington (a two-barrelled metallic cartridge version), the Sharps' four-barrelled pistol, and the Williamson.

The Williamson had a sliding barrel, which was pushed forward to load either a steel case with a nipple for use as a percussion pistol, or to load a proper rimfire cartridge. This popular pistol was also the favourite 'hideout' weapon of Wild Bill Hickok, 'the Prince of Pistoleers', who carried a pair in his waistcoat pockets.

Naturally, with the development of such deadly and efficient pocket and belt pistols, it was only a matter of time before the innumerable multi-shot weapons gave way to a practical form of 'revolving pistol'. Thanks to the percussion lock, such weapons soon became a reality.

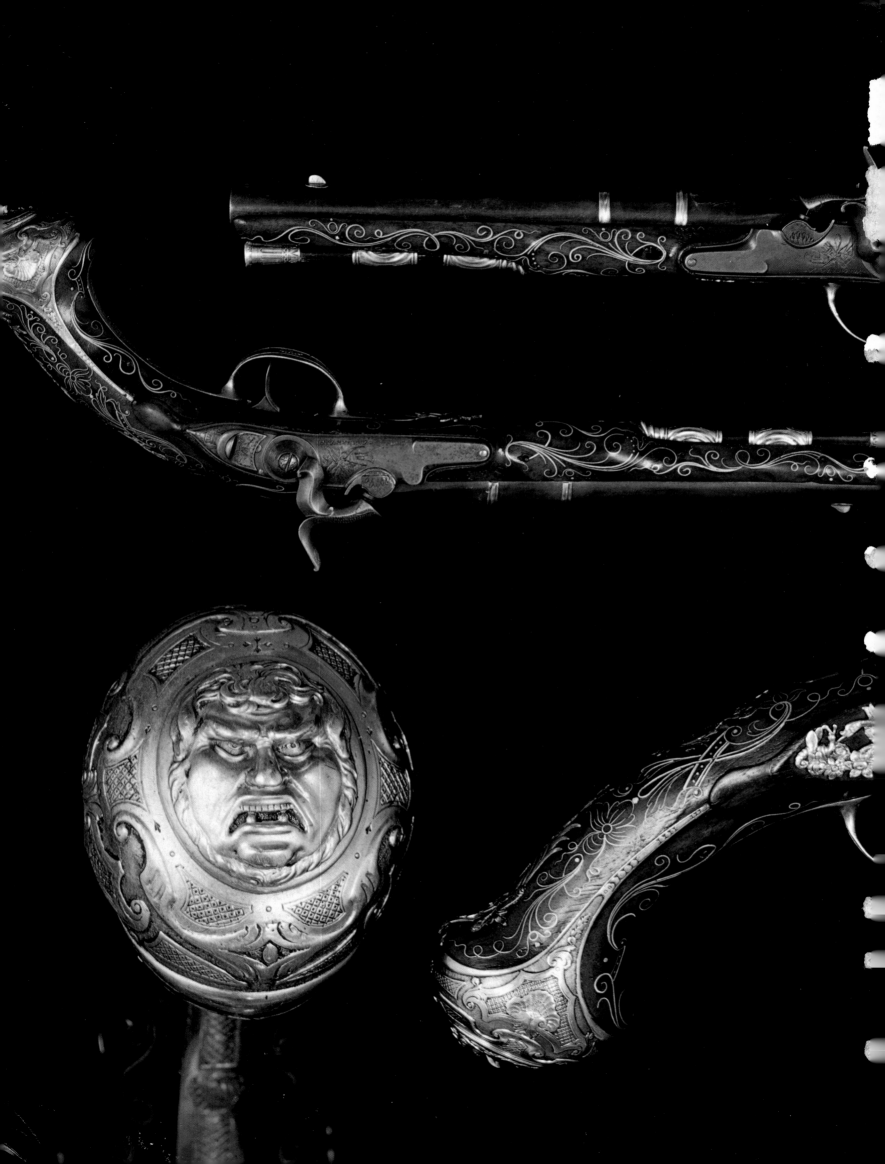

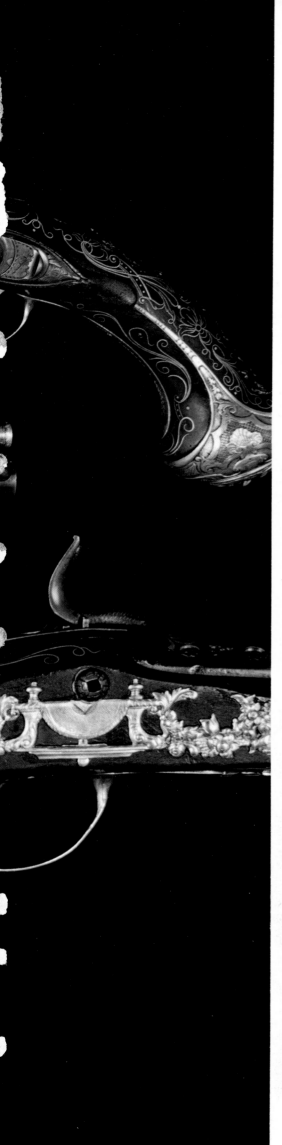

Left This magnificent pair of pistols was made by John Harman of London in 1729 for the young Frederick the Great. Beautifully mounted with silver, the escutcheon plates are in gold. In about 1830 the pistols were converted to percussion, yet they still have something of their original splendour. The original locks have been retained and only the hammers and nipples have been added at a later date.

Below Specimens of Forsyth's pistols are rare and cased sets are even more scarce. This set dates from around 1811 and is complete with accessories, including two spare mainsprings.

Of interest to collectors is the label pasted in the lid of the box. This gives full instructions about loading, dismantling and cleaning the weapons.

Bottom Joseph Egg's successors continued to make fine arms well into the 19th century, and the meticulous detail of their workmanship is shown in this splendid pair of pocket pistols (*c.* 1830). The stocks are inlaid with silver, which in turn has been finely engraved. Like other pistols of the day, the triggers fold away into the weapons when not in use. Once the hammer is pulled to full cock, the trigger drops down for use.

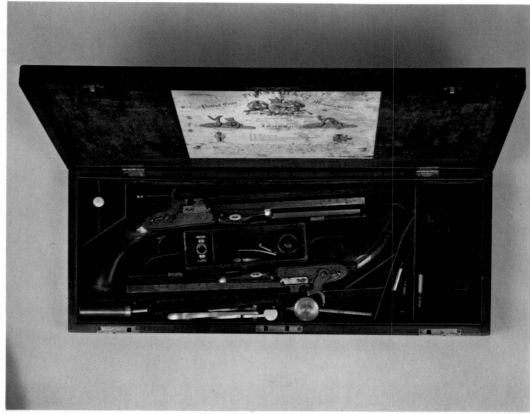

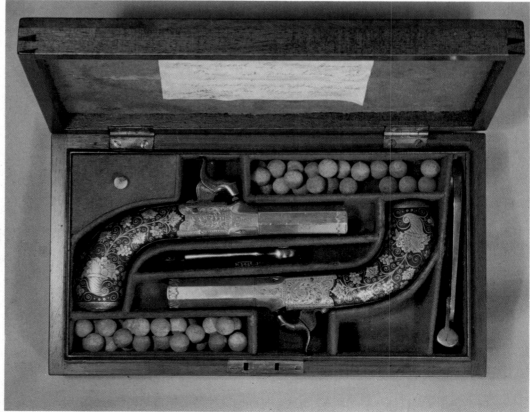

Far left Brun of Paris made this beautiful pair of percussion target pistols *c.* 1845. The carved stocks are of ebony, and the finely worked barrels and lock plates have been gilded. Many long hours went into the preparation of the moulds to produce parts of such pistols and accessories.

Left The original Sam Browne belt, percussion pistols and medals of General Sir Samuel Browne V.C. (1824–1901). He won his award in the Indian Mutiny, but is best remembered for the sword belt he invented for himself, which later became standard officers' wear when in Service Dress. It was compulsory for British officers and warrant officers up to 1939, when it became optional. The belt was adopted by many armies.

Right A pair of target pistols, made by Bekker and Rawscher of Warsaw. They are tastefully decorated and fitted with the spur trigger guard that was a popular feature of most Continental manufacturers in the mid-19th century.

Below The Parisian maker, Henri le Page, excelled himself with this beautiful pistol, made in 1837 for King Louis-Phillipe. The elaborately carved stock is solid ivory. The finely chiselled steel barrel and trigger-guard (on which the maker's name is inscribed) are inlaid with gold.

Left Four specimens of Deringer's pocket pistols. Top left is the large 4½-inch barrelled .45 calibre pistol fitted with a ramrod. Top right is a .45 calibre 3-inch version. Bottom left is the more familiar 2-inch barrelled pistol (of the type that killed Lincoln) in .44 calibre; and at bottom right is another 3-inch barrelled weapon but equipped with a ramrod. Henry Deringer's little pocket pistols were widely copied.

Below left By 1855, Colt's revolvers were well established, and his Dragoon or Holster pistol was regarded as a fashionable weapon. Yet the U.S. Government still issued its mounted troops with this monstrous single-shot Springfield pistol carbine. The stock could be detached and carried on a lanyard, while the pistol was put in a saddle holster.

Right The popularity of the pocket pistols of Henry Deringer greatly influenced other makers, but, as can be seen from this assortment of weapons, the large-calibre pocket pistol was far from new. At the bottom on either side are a pair of ivory-stocked, folding-trigger, box-lock percussion pistols of the 1840s. Centre left is a Remington over-and-under, a Derringer that was popular well into this century. Above it is a Colt's Second Model .41 Derringer and, at the top, the unique Sharps' four-barrel rimfire pistol. A spring-loaded firing pin turned on a ratchet each time it was cocked to bring it in line with each of the four barrels in turn. Of the two pistols in the middle that on the left is a typical pocket pistol of the 1830–40s, and the other is the Colt's Third Model Derringer, designed by F. Alexander Thuer. When the pistol is set at half-cock the breech end of the barrel is twisted to the right for loading or ejecting. These small but lethal weapons were very popular in Britain in the 1870s. Centre right is a fine flintlock box-lock over-and-under tap-action pistol, *c*. 1810. The small lever at the side controls a steel drum which opens and closes the vents to each barrel. Above it is a fine cannon-barrelled pocket pistol of the 1780s. Among the accessories are a nipple wrench, oil-bottle, bullet mould, powder flask, and four .41 rimfire bullets for a Thuer No. 3.

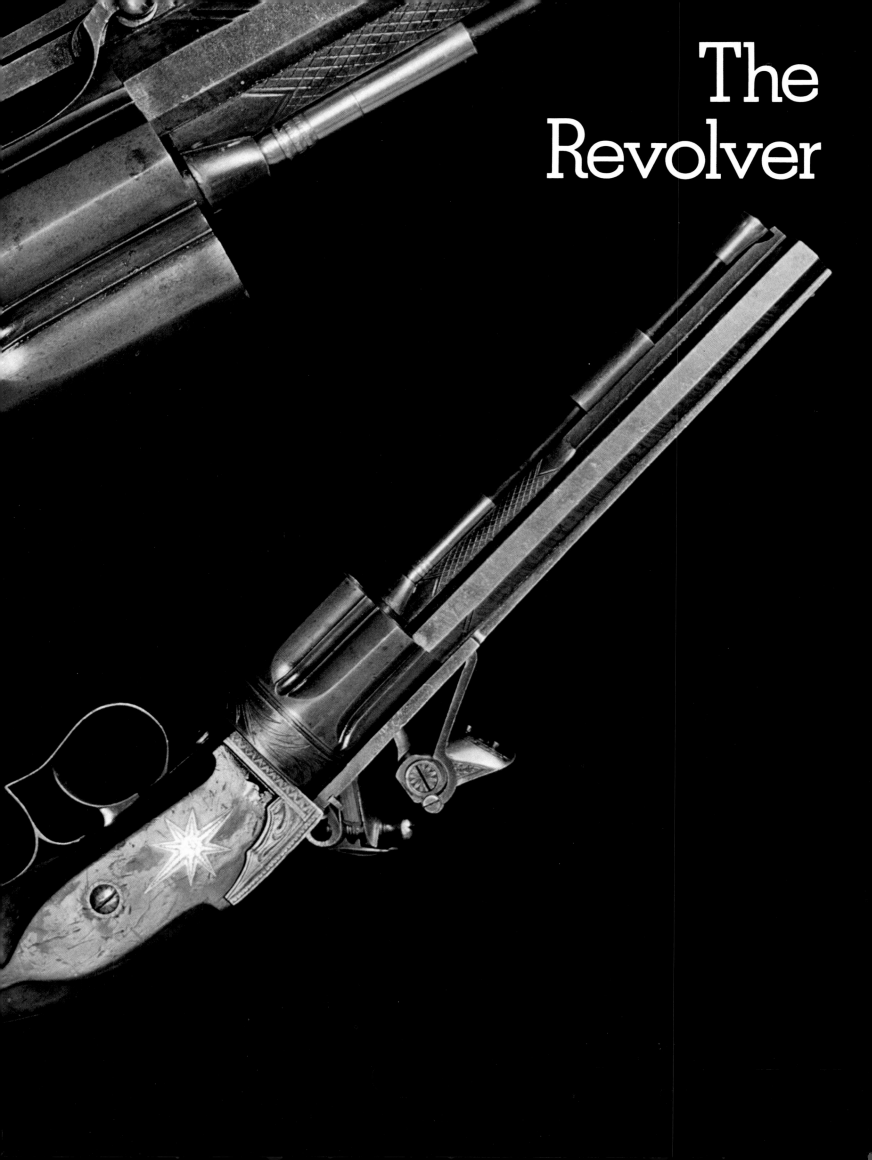

The
Revolver

Way out West it was said that 'a Colt makes all men equal', hence the cowboy name for a pistol–an equalizer. A skinny weakling could stand up to a human gorilla if he had learnt how to handle a shootin' iron, and the chances were that the 'iron' was a Colt.

Yet revolvers did not originate in the American Wild West. The idea of a multi-fire hand weapon had obsessed inventors for centuries, but nobody had come up with a practical answer. During the sixteenth and seventeenth centuries, experiments were made with various forms of matchlocks and wheel-locks, and other arms with revolving barrels (including revolving carbines), but none were really successful. There is even a famous seventeenth-century English snaphaunce with a revolving breech, which predates the better publicized products of the nineteenth century.

In 1818, Elisha Collier, a citizen of Boston, sailed to Britain with a revolving-breeched flintlock pistol. How much of this invention was his own and how much he owed to Captain Artemus Wheeler of Concord, Massachusetts, is debatable. Some, indeed, have claimed that both Americans got the idea from an Englishman named James

pistol was tried again–without achieving any notable success.

Collier's revolver naturally inspired many imitators, one of which proved very popular. This was the multi-barrelled pistol known as the 'pepperbox'. Early specimens of this unwieldly pistol were hand-turned, but in later versions the lifting of the hammer by pressure applied to the trigger also turned the barrels. Understandably, the pepperbox was most unreliable. Mark Twain, during a stagecoach trip out West in 1861, was perturbed by the slap-happy shooting antics of a fellow traveller and pointed out that the barrels of his 'Allen' pepperbox were liable to go off all at once. In fact one wild shot brought down a mule standing some 30 yards from where he was aiming. The unfortunate marksman did not want the mule, 'but the owner came out with a double-barrelled shotgun and persuaded him to buy it anyhow!'

It was the American Samuel Colt who finally produced the first practical and reliable revolver. In 1835, he patented the design in England, and a year later in the U.S.A. The system was amazingly simple, yet ingenious. The cylinder or breech revolved on an axis,

ABOVE *Having been a cowboy, the artist Charles Russell (1864–1926) drew on his experiences in depicting typical scenes of the Wild West. This famous picture,* When Guns Speak, Death Settles Disputes, *shows a bunch of cowboys shooting it out with local gamblers after hitting town. Although such gunfights were quite common from 1865 until the end of the century, the death toll was not anything like as heavy as Hollywood would have us believe!*
PREVIOUS PAGES *Though Elisha Collier's flintlock and percussion lock revolving pistols did not meet with official approval, they have since been found in sufficient numbers to show that they sold well. This fine specimen dates from the early 1820s. The close-up view of the cylinder and cock shows how tension was maintained on the periphery of the cylinder by the spring bearing down upon it.*

Puckle, whose work will be discussed in a later chapter. In any event, Collier received the credit and it was his 'revolver' which was patented in England on 24 November 1818. Basically it consisted of a fixed barrel, beneath which was an axis on which revolved a cylinder or breech. This was moved around by a spiral spring like that of a watch, and was activated by a toothed wheel and a catch worked by the lock motions. The mouth of each chamber was recessed, so that when a spring at the rear of the cylinder pushed it forward, it fitted over the breech of the barrel, forming a gas seal when the pistol was discharged. In the opinion of the English Select Committee, who tried the weapon out at Woolwich, the mechanism was too complicated. So the automatic turning mechanism was dispensed with, a percussion lock was substituted for a flint lock, and the

or spindle attached to the barrel, which in turn was held on by a wedge. Each time the hammer was pulled back, a hand or pawl attached to it turned the cylinder, so that a chamber lined up with the bore.

The earliest Colt's revolvers were five-shooters. They were made at an armoury at Paterson, New Jersey, and are today known as 'Colt Patersons'. Despite some successful bloodletting in the wars against the Seminole Indians of Florida, and long service with the Texas Navy (when the state was independent) and the Texas Rangers, by the early 1840s the Paterson venture was over. But in 1846, at the insistence of Captain Samuel Walker, a former Texas Ranger, and now a captain in the U.S. Regiment of Mounted Rifles, the U.S. Government ordered 1,000 revolvers from Colt for use in its war of expansion against Mexico. In view of Walker's criticism of the Paterson revolver, Colt redesigned it. In place of the folding trigger previously used, he fitted a standard trigger guard and simplified the action. It is worth noting that this 'single-action' mechanism (in which the hammer had to be thumb-cocked for each shot) is still employed today in Colt's Single Action Army, or Peacemaker, revolvers.

The success of the new revolver, known to history as the Colt-Walker Dragoon, quickly led to new orders, and Colt built a factory in his home town of Hartford, Connecticut. During the Crimean War, he set up another factory in London where he produced thousands of his Navy model revolvers for sale to the British Government.

Successors to the Walker revolver included a modified version, the

1848 Dragoon, followed by the 1848 and 1849 pocket pistols, the 1851 and 1861 Navy revolvers and the 1860 Army revolver. There was a steady demand for these and similar weapons, for this was an age in which a man without a pistol was not considered properly dressed. Consequently Sam Colt reigned supreme in his field until he died in 1862. The most successful pistol produced during his lifetime was the 1851 Navy revolver. Wild Bill Hickok, perhaps the only gunfighter whose life matched his legend, carried a pair of these revolvers through most of his career, wearing them butt forward in belt or holsters for the reverse draw that was so popular on the Plains.

Colt had many rivals. On the Continent, the Frenchman, Casimir Lefaucheux had pioneered the famous pinfire system in the early 1850s and this was quickly adopted by the French Government. The cartridge had a metal base, a paper or metal tube containing a powder charge, and a conical bullet. Seated in the base of the cartridge was a percussion pellet attached to a small pin, which protruded from the side of the case. When struck by the hammer, this pin detonated the charge. Examples of the pinfire system were shown at the Great Exhibition in 1851, but the pinfire was not popular in Britain.

Robert Adams, the London gunsmith, whose revolver was patented in 1851, was Colt's main English rival. He developed a percussion cartridge for his pistol, which was inserted into the chamber by thumb pressure alone. This proved impracticable because the charges were frequently shaken loose when the revolvers were carried on horseback. Later, a more reliable ramming system was incorporated to seat the ball firmly into the chamber.

The key difference between the Colt and the Adams was in their actions. Whereas Colt's hammer had to be cocked by the thumb for each shot, Adams used a self-cocking action, similar to the old pepperboxes, so that it only required pressure on the trigger to cock and fire. Unfortunately, it lacked accuracy and was thought to be dangerous when fired from horseback; and it was not until 1855 that Adams was considered a serious rival to Colt. In that year the mechanism was improved by the inclusion of Lieutenant Beaumont's double and single action, which enables the Adams to be cocked either by the thumb or by pressure on the trigger.

Colt's American rivals included Remington (who also pioneered the typewriter and the sewing machine in the 1870s) and, later, Smith and Wesson. This team obtained the exclusive rights to produce bored-through cylinders to take metallic ammunition under a patent granted to Rollin White in 1855. As early as 1857, Smith and Wesson were producing small-calibred rimfire revolvers. The odd situation whereby they alone had the right to produce commercial breech-loading metallic cartridge revolvers in the U.S.A. lasted until the patent expired in 1869.

In Europe, where no such restrictions existed, various forms of fixed ammunition were being used in the early 1860s and within a few years the percussion revolver had largely been replaced. Yet until the late 1870s, some British Army officers were still using percussion pistols because of the unreliable state of metallic ammunition at that time.

The most famous Colt revolver was the Single Action Army model of 1873, known as the Peacemaker or the Frontier. In the .45-calibre version it remained the standard sidearm of the U.S. Cavalry until 1890. Among its principal competitors were the Smith and Wesson 'American' and 'Russian' models (the latter developed for Czarist Russia), their Schofield revolver, and Remington's new Model Army revolver of 1875.

Meanwhile, European makers produced many improvements to the basic revolver design, and in London John Adams, believed to be a cousin of Robert, patented several revolvers in the late 1850s and early 1860s, which achieved some success. But most popular of all was his 1867 model. Following several modifications, it was used by the British Army until the late 1870s. Both his 1867 and 1872 models were used, but not frequently fired, by the North-West Mounted Police. Unlike law enforcement officers below the border, the Mounties seldom had to shoot their man. The Webley family in Birmingham produced a number of notable weapons, and by the 1880s had

merged with W. C. Scott to form the now world-famous firm of Webley and Scott.

Whether revolvers were made in Britain, Europe, the U.S.A., Japan or Russia, their use was always dictated by necessity and practicability. In Britain the Army had experimented with Colt's revolvers as a means of rearming infantry as early as 1852; and in 1854 it tested the Navy Dragoon models at distances of over 400 yards, with good results. But it was soon realized that few soldiers could be expected to be as accurate as experts. So the revolver was reduced in status to a secondary weapon, and was chiefly used by officers and mounted troops.

The United States, by tradition, retained the revolver as an indispensable personal asset, and even today it has a place in military thinking. But its greatest fame was on the Frontier, where it played a major role in formulating the myth of the Wild West.

The simplicity and reliability of the revolver have led to its being retained as the principal weapon of many of the world's police forces, despite the introduction of more sophisticated hand guns, such as the automatic pistol, which will be discussed in a later chapter.

Even as the revolver was being developed, great progress was being made in the improvement of a weapon which, from a military point of view, was the most important of all – the rifle. But before dealing with this vital development we must take a brief trip back in time to see what had been going on in non-military circles, where men shot only for pleasure and profit.

Three military revolvers. At the top is the Tranter Service pistol of 1878, a .45-calibre revolver which retained the loading gate and rod ejection system but was double-action. Only a limited number of these revolvers were purchased by the British Government. In the centre is a fine Beaumont Adams revolver, model of 1855–6, fitted with the Kerr rammer, adopted by the British Government in 1856 to replace the Colt's Navy revolver, model of 1851, which had been purchased in bulk for the Crimean War. It survived until the 1870s, when many were converted to centre fire ammunition. At the bottom is the immortal Colt Single-Action Army revolver, model of 1873, otherwise known as the Peacemaker. This one is nickel-plated and fitted with hard rubber or guttapercha grips. In its original calibre of .45 it was known as the 'Cavalry' model and fitted with a 7½-in barrel. Similarly calibred weapons with 5½-in barrel lengths were 'Artillery' pistols, while 4¾-in barrelled weapons were the 'Civilian' model. In 1878, to cater for owners of Winchester 1873 .44–40 rifles (in which a .44-calibre bullet was propelled by 40 grains of powder), the Colt company produced the famous .44–40 'Frontier Six-Shooter' version of the Single Action Army. The Peacemaker is the most popular revolver ever made. Manufactured from 1873 until 1941, it was revived in 1955 and is still in production.

Left Colt's .36 calibre six-shot Navy revolver was the favourite pistol of soldier, plainsman, cowboy and bandit prior to the introduction of the Peacemaker. Some 215,000 of them were manufactured in Hartford between 1850 and 1873. This is a fine specimen of the version produced at Colt's London Armoury between 1853–6. The pistol is complete in its original box with a cleaning rod, bullet mould, nipple wrench, powder flask and cap box. The small compartment behind the butt contains spare nipples and a spare mainspring. The London-made Colt's revolvers had iron backstraps and trigger guards, whereas the American pistols used brass ones. The surface of the cylinder has a rolled-on engraving of ships in battle. In 1848 Colt produced his .31-calibre Baby Dragoon, a pocket revolver based on the recent Walker and Dragoon pistols. It proved so popular that in 1849 the pistol was modified and remained in production with slight variations until 1873, by which time approximately 315,000 had been produced in Hartford. This is the London version, with iron trigger guard and back-strap, in its original case, complete with accessories. The engraving on the cylinder of the pocket pistol is of a stage-coach hold-up.

Top right The Colt Walker Dragoon. This remarkable 'cannon' was manufactured for Samuel Colt by Eli Whitney Jr, of Whitneyville, Connecticut, in 1847. Colt did not have his own factory at the time, for the Paterson venture had failed several years before. The war with Mexico in 1846 had revived interest in Colt's arms, and Samuel Walker's criticism of the earlier Paterson pistols led to Colt producing this massive .44 calibre 9-inch barrelled six-shot weapon. The pistol weighed 4 lbs 9 oz, and fired a 219-grain lead bullet backed by 50 grains of black powder at a muzzle velocity believed by experts to have been at least 1,500 feet per second! Walker said that the pistol was as effective as a rifle at 100 yards and superior to a musket at 200 yards. Some 1,100 of these pistols were made, but they were short-lived, for they were so powerful that some are known to have blown up.

Centre right The Colt Texas Paterson Holster Pistol. This is a fine cased example of one of Sam Colt's earliest model revolvers. These pistols were manufactured during the 1830s and appeared in several sizes and calibres. The five-shot Holster Pistol illustrated is .36 calibre, with a 9-inch barrel.

Bottom right The .44 Calibre Colt Third Model 1848 Hartford Dragoon or Holster pistol was developed from the Walker, and this specimen is a superb example of the engraver's art. The close relief engraving and finely chiselled inlay and gold figures are typical of the workmanship reserved for very special presentation arms. Weapons similar to this were presented in 1854 by Colt to the Czar of Russia and the Sultan of Turkey.

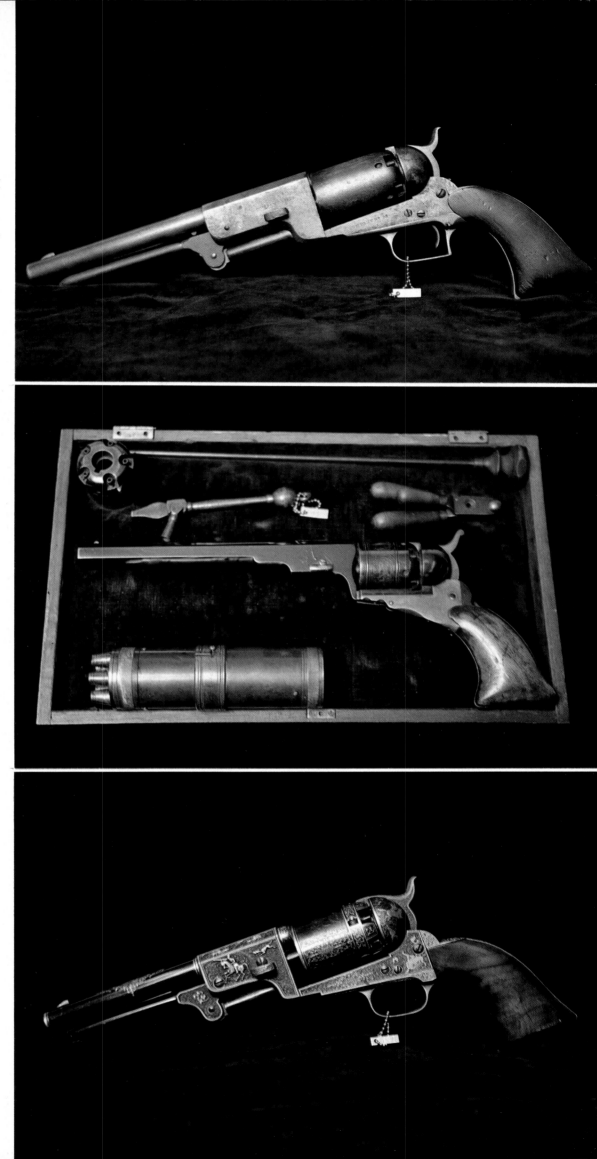

Below An ornate pistol by William Tranter of Birmingham, perhaps the finest of the early British revolver makers. Basically the same in appearance as the Adams (Tranter made some of the early Adams pistols under contract), it differs in its mechanism. To cock and fire the pistol, the spur projecting from the base of the guard is pulled back, and this action cocks the hammer. To release it and fire the pistol, the trigger is squeezed in the normal way. Complicated though it may seem, Tranter's 1853 patented design proved very popular. Allan Pinkerton, the Scottish-born founder of the most famous detective agency in the U.S.A., is said to have armed his men with this weapon. *Right* Collier's revolving breech mechanisms were followed by other similar systems. This 'pepperbox' by Joseph Lang of London is dated *c*. 1850 and is the most common type. The barrels are turned when the trigger is pulled, and at the same time the hammer raises and drops onto the cap. To protect the caps from damage or from falling off, the nipples are housed in a rim or cuplike projection at the front of the frame. Although their accuracy and reliability left much to be desired, pepperboxes flooded the market from the 1830s to the mid 1860s. *Below right* The British gunmaker, Robert Adams, patented his revolver in 1851. In the same year it was displayed at the Great Exhibition in London alongside Colonel

Samuel Colt's revolver, both types arousing keen interest. This version of Adams' 1851 model is unusual in that the butt is plain varnished. Normally, the wood was finely checkered to ensure a firmer grip. It is self-cocking so that the hammer is cocked and fired by the trigger. Later versions were fitted with the Beaumont lock, which allowed either for self-cocking or for cocking by thumb for single-action working.

Loading Procedure for Cap and Ball Revolvers
Percussion revolvers are frequently called 'muzzle-loaders', but they were not actually loaded at the muzzle of the barrel, but at the front of the cylinder. The pistol was set at half cock so that the cylinder could spin freely. Next, a measured charge of powder from a flask was poured into each chamber. A round ball or conical (pointed) bullet was then placed in the mouth of each chamber and forced in with a rammer, fixed underneath or alongside the barrel. Prepared ammunition (paper, skin or tinfoil cartridges), containing powder and ball, was also available, which saved time. Once each chamber was loaded, a small copper cap filled with a fulminate (usually mercury) was then slipped over the nipple or cone at the rear of the chamber. The revolver was then ready for use. Modern black powder shooters often smear the loaded chamber mouths with grease to help reduce fouling.

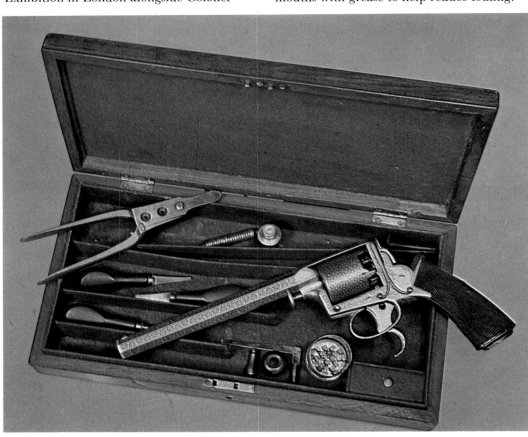

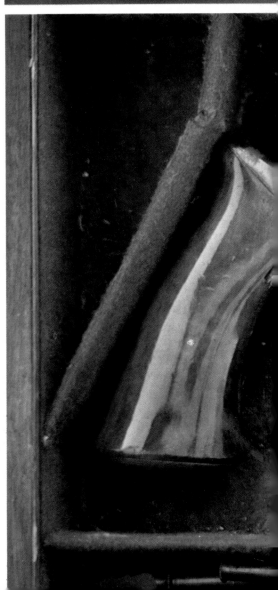

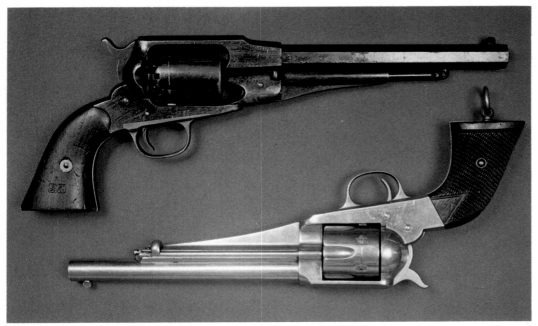

Left By the late 1860s, European gunmakers were concentrating on metallic ammunition, and the days of the percussion pistol were numbered. In the United States, however, both types were still widely used. Two of Remington's most popular weapons are shown here. The percussion revolver is the New Model Army of 1863 and the fine nickel-plated pistol is the famous model of 1875. The similarity of the latter to the Colt New Model Army of 1873 caused a stir, but the Remington was considered inferior to its Colt rival.

Below The London gunmaker, John Adams, patented this revolver in 1866. Although it was perhaps the finest of all English percussion revolvers, it came too late, for already both the military and public were clamouring for metallic cartridge arms. In the mid-1870s many thousands of percussion revolvers were converted to cartridge, so unconverted specimens like this cased example are now quite rare.

Right Three British Army revolvers of the late 18th century. At the top is the John Adams revolver of 1867, a popular weapon (chambered for the .450 short cartridge invented by Colonel Boxer) which, in 1869, proved superior to the Colt Thuer conversion in trials at Woolwich. Improvements to it resulted in the famous John Adams model of 1872, shown centre. Like its predecessor, the 1872 model was a true double-action pistol, but had the same defect of being slow-loading, relying on a gate to load the cart-ridges and a rod to eject them. In the Enfield Mark II revolver, below, which replaced it, an ejection system was incorporated, speeding up loading and unloading.

Left Colt's main rivals in the United States were Smith and Wesson, who began producing bored-through cylinder revolvers (firing metallic cartridges instead of the normal cap and ball loads) in 1857. Illustrated at the top is the second Smith and Wesson model, a .22 seven-shot pistol produced in the 1850s. At the bottom is the .32-calibre version with birdhead grips. Of the two large weapons in the centre, the upper one is the No. 3 Model 'American' .44 six-shooter, a later version of the No. 3 American model that first appeared in 1870. When the catch at the rear of the recoil shield was raised, the barrel dropped down and forced up the cylinder ratchet, which included the extractor, pushing out the spent cases. The lower weapon with the spur on the guard is the famous 'Russian' model, thousands of which were sold to the Imperial Russian Government, including ammunition to their specifications.

Right An interesting group of Smith and Wesson revolvers: at the top is a .44 calibre New Model No. 3 (American) which is engraved and silver-plated, with ivory grips. Below it is an ornate gold-plated and engraved example of the double-action revolver *c.* 1880. Note the monogrammed pearl grips. The flanking weapons are a fine pair of .22 calibre rimfire No. 1½ Second Model revolvers. The barrels tip up to allow loading and unloading, and the spent cases are ejected by means of the rod shown projecting from beneath the barrel.

Below right A fine cased specimen of the Smith and Wesson .32 rimfire No. 2 Army revolver. First issued in June 1861, it proved to be a popular weapon, and a pair of pistols very similar to this one were presented to Brevet Major General George A. Custer in 1869. It has been alleged, but never proved, that Wild Bill Hickok was carrying a No. 2 as a 'hide-out' gun when he was killed in 1876.

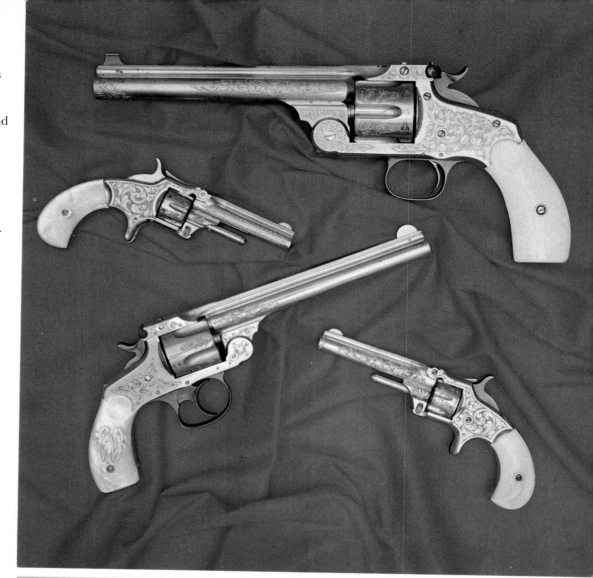

Left By the 1880s, Colt's revolvers had undergone many changes. At the top of this group is the 1878 double-action Army, an improved version of the 1877 Lightning, but with a solid frame. The poor quality of the lockwork, however, was much criticized. Urged to produce a good double-action, self-extracting revolver, Colt's came up, in 1889, with the first of their swing-out cylinder arms. By 1892, the manufacture date of the weapon in the centre, it had become popular both for military and law-enforcing purposes. The weapon at the bottom, shown with the cylinder swung out, is the famous New Service revolver, some 335,000 of which were made between 1898 and 1944. Thanks to its balance and weight of frame it was very accurate.

Below A side view of the Colt double-action, swing-out cylinder model of 1892. The bar at the rear of the cylinder is pushed, releasing

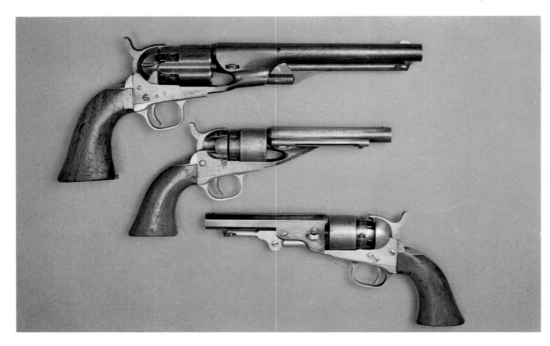

the cylinder which swings down on a crank. The spindle underneath the barrel is pushed in, operating the ejector at the rear of the chambers. This method of loading and unloading was a considerable improvement on Colt's previous systems.

Bottom left Among Colonel Samuel Colt's many pistols was the famous New Model Army revolver of 1860, which proved so popular in the American Civil War (1861–5). The pistol underwent several changes, and the specimen illustrated at the top is an early one (No. 210), which had flutes cut into the cylinder to reduce weight. Later models were made with rounded cylinders, complete with the roll engraving found on the earlier Navy revolvers. The frame used on these pistols was identical to that of the .36-calibre 1851 Navy pistol. To increase the calibre to .44 the front end of the cylinder was enlarged, and the frame milled

to take what was called a 'rebated' cylinder. Below the Colt 1860 are two pocket pistols produced on the same principle. Their basic frames were designed for the .31-calibre model of 1849, but the pistols were increased in calibre to .36. The upper pistol is an 1862 Police pistol converted to .38 rimfire, and the lower one a standard Pocket Pistol of Navy calibre.

Right In 1894, the Colt Company introduced a special target version of the Peacemaker, the Bisley, in honour of the world-famous shooting ranges in Surrey, England. It differed basically from the standard model in that the hammer was sloped back and the handle was longer and more steeply curved. On the right is a standard 5½-in barrelled Single-Action Army revolver, *c.* 1875, alongside a 7½-in targeted version of the Bisley, the loading gate of which is open, exposing the rear of the chamber.

Left At bottom left is the Webley .455 Mark II, and to its right the Webley-Fosbery. The automatic pistol at the bottom right is the famous .455 Webley Self-Loading model, once the official sidearm of the Royal Navy. Above these is the .455 target revolver, and at the top, the Mark V No. 1.

Top right Two versions of the Enfield revolver No. 2 Mark I. Above is the .38-calibre 1931 model (standard British service revolver of World War II), a six-shot double-action weapon with a built-in safety device that makes the hammer rebound away from the cartridges after firing. Below is an interesting cutaway version that conveys some idea of how the pistol works. On the side is the lever which controls the stirrup, just in front of the hammer. Once released, it enables the barrel to drop down to eject or reload the chambers.

Centre right A collection of Italian revolvers and automatics. At top left is the so-called 'System Bodego', the six-shot, double-action frame model of 1889, in 10.35mm centre-fire, equipped with the folding trigger so popular on the Continent. This particular weapon was made by the Royal Fabrica d'Armi Glisenti at Brescia. To the right is a later version with a normal trigger guard and a rounded barrel. At lower left are two early Beretta weapons, and, on the right, a Glisenti automatic together with a flare pistol, all relics of the World Wars.

Bottom right Flare pistols are standard equipment on land and at sea, vital for communication and rescue operations. Here, together with wirecutters and other trenching tools of World War I, are two examples by Webley.

Below This fine .455-calibre specimen of the famous Webley-Fosbery semi-automatic revolver was a milestone in arms development. The barrel, receiver and cylinder form a unit which moves backwards and forwards in grooves cut in the frame, these parts recoiling when the weapon is fired. The pistol is cocked for the first shot and the recoil activates the cocking mechanism for the successive shots.

Sporting Guns

Hunting was the sport of kings long before racing also received the accolade, and commoners have been enjoying it too, legally or illegally, since time immemorial. But although it was a logical progression from bow, spear and javelin to gun, the outcome was a revolution in man's attitudes to the handling and possession of arms. For whereas the yeoman had been encouraged to practise with his bow and other weapons, so as to be ready for war, only the nobility or the well-to-do could afford, or were encouraged, to buy and use guns.

The use of firearms by robbers and outlaws in England during the reign of Henry VIII led to an Act of Parliament in 1542 which declared that malicious, or:

the local bands of smugglers and wreckers on the sea shore.

Nevertheless, as the years passed, these regulations were relaxed or modified. Throughout Europe more and more guns were made to cater for sportsmen and poachers alike. As the cost of firearms decreased so they ceased to be a symbol of class distinction.

From the time of the first matchlocks, weapons had been made for hunting. Long-barrelled fowling pieces were very popular, and whereas most hunters restricted their activities to open spaces and woodlands, many were prosecuted for using firearms too close to towns and villages. By the seventeenth century, 'birding', as it was called, knew no social barriers, and even poorer people engaged in it. But the motives were often different. The rich engaged in it for

'evill disposed myndes and purposes have wilfully and shamefully comytted, perpetrated and done diverse detestible and shamefull murthers, robberies, felonyees, ryotts and routes with Crossbowes, lyttle shorte handguns, and little hagbutts, to the great perill and contynual fear and daunger of the Kings most lovinge subjects . . .'

It was forbidden to shoot or keep one of these weapons in the house unless the owner had lands or an income exceeding £100, a classic case of one law for the rich and another for the poor. Naturally this restricted possession and use to the nobility, gentry and prosperous, newly emerging middle classes. The only exceptions to this rule were inhabitants of coastal areas who were allowed to buy and practise with guns, presumably to repel everyone from the king's enemies to

ABOVE *One visitor to the American West, before the white settlers arrived, was the German naturalist Prince Maximilian of Wied (second from right in the foreground), who was accompanied by the Swiss artist, Karl Bodmer (right). Maximilian's fascinating book about his journey* Travels in the Interior of North America, *published in several languages in the late 1830s and early 1840s, was magnificently supplemented by Bodmer's bound portfolio of polychrome engravings. This one shows a meeting of the two travellers with Minataree Indians at Fort Union, on the Upper Missouri, in 1833–4. The Prince's party, incidentally, did not use their guns, as did the early visitors, to slaughter local wildlife.*

PREVIOUS PAGES *A detail of the le Bourgeoys gun shown on pages 66–7, showing the royal crown and L, together with superb inlay and fine figure engravings. Time has made very little impact on this gun, and it is in remarkably good condition.*

sports, but the poor were frequently forced to do it to protect their crops.

To cater for what was clearly a growing and lucrative market, English gunmakers produced a weapon which was in its way unique. This was the famous 'birding piece', a massive smoothbore gun with a barrel which was sometimes five or six feet long. Evidently the reasoning in some circles was that the longer the gun, the greater the range. Ballistically, this was not so, because of a breaking action induced by the friction of the ball on the bore. However, the long barrels did give maximum propulsion from a slow-burning charge. The results seemed impressive, and the long barrels were retained. As the quality of powder was improved barrels were shortened, but even when shorter-barrelled weapons became very popular (especially among poachers and other criminals who had to operate in a confined space and with the utmost secrecy), the long-barrelled weapons were still fashionable. The principle was followed in the military sphere, and very long-barrelled weapons were used to defend castles and manors in the English Civil War.

Each new generation introduced new ideas and inventions. The popularity of hunting, and its patronage by Louis XIII of France and other monarchs, did much to promote increased interest in shooting, and by the eighteenth century the flintlock fowling piece had become an object of beauty and fine balance which earned it a place in the forefront of sporting weapons well into the nineteenth century. Once the percussion lock became generally accepted, so too did new sporting guns which made use of it, and a new word appeared in the English language – the 'shotgun'.

In little more than a century since its introduction, the shotgun has gained a reputation hardly equalled by any other weapon. The reason for this notoriety is to be found in its basic purpose; unlike most weapons which fire only one ball or bullet, the shotgun is designed to fire a number of shots, or lead pellets, the length of the barrel and the choke (a constriction at the mouth of the barrel to control the spread of shot) determining the pattern in which the pellets fall. When employed as originally intended, for sport, at the correct range, game is mutilated no more than is necessary.

Nevertheless, other uses were soon found for the shotgun. In the late eighteenth century and early nineteenth century, a number of weapons had been produced with belled muzzles and were known as 'blunderbusses'. Mailcoach guards regularly carried them, and since their ammunition was popularly believed to contain as many old horseshoe nails as pellets, people were wary of them. The appearance of the shotgun, however, revived interest in spread-shot weapons, and as early as the 1850s, sawn-off shotguns were being employed for a variety of purposes, including war. They were used in the bloody Kansas-Missouri border wars of the 1850s, where the pro- and anti-slavery factions did their best to exterminate each other, and also against Sepoys in the Indian Mutiny. In the West, Wells Fargo armed its conductors or stagecoach 'messengers' with these singularly unpleasant weapons and thus the 'shotgun guard' was born.

As a personal weapon it was greatly prized. John H. Holliday, better known as Doc Holliday, who sided with the Earps in the famous gunfight at Tombstone's O.K. Corral, carried a shotgun, which had been made by W. W. Greener to his own specifications. The weapon which had been designed for sportsmen soon came to be the hallmark of the bank robber and the gangster.

Although few of the nineteenth century inventors who tried to improve the accuracy of the sporting guns had as much success as the Reverend Forsyth of Belhevie, such experiments did eventually lead to the adoption of rifled arms, which had been tried out as early as the sixteenth century. Rifled arms were, at first, very expensive, and not really appreciated by the average hunter and sportsman. In Germany and other parts of Europe, however, sporting guns with rifled barrels became commonplace. The most important of these were the Jaegers, made with very heavy barrels. The ball was so tight that it had to be hammered into the rifling; but once loaded, the gun proved highly accurate and was greatly prized.

The United States produced a number of famous sporting, hunting

and other rifles that helped to revolutionize military and non-military techniques. The Plains rifle, for example, like many contemporary models used by hunting and shooting enthusiasts, fired a round ball, which could easily be damaged or badly seated during loading. The army, however, preferred the conical bullet.

Amongst the most popular Plains rifle was the Hawken, a light weapon which resembled the famous flintlock Kentucky rifle, except that it worked by percussion. There were also heavier-calibred weapons used for hunting buffalo. Unlike the Kentucky and Hawken rifles, with their graceful lines, such weapons were designed simply for practical purposes. The barrels were very heavy, usually octagonal in shape, and the calibres ranged from .45 to .56. The stock was thick, short and devoid of decoration. Yet for accuracy and killing power, the Plains rifle had few rivals.

Perhaps the most famous of all the Plains rifles were those made by Christian Sharps. His early breechloaders will be discussed later, but his greatest rifle was the 'Big Fifty', a .50-calibre buffalo gun. This could kill a buffalo at a mile, yet ironically, it was not introduced until about 1880. By then, most of the buffalo had been decimated by hunters, thus depriving the Plains Indians of food, shelter, clothing

In the 1830s the American artist, George Catlin, made an incomparable pictorial record of the West, including scenes of Indians and early plainsmen hunting buffalo. Occasionally, as in this picture, Chasing Back, *things could go unexpectedly wrong for the hunter.*

and other essentials, and contributing to their downfall. The 'Big Fifty' appeared just as the remaining buffalo were being saved from extinction by legislation.

Man's attitude to hunting and shooting for sport and pleasure has lately undergone a distinct change. In the late nineteenth and early twentieth centuries, sportsmen killed a vast quantity of game and wildlife in Africa and North America. Hunters returning from a good 'shoot' calculated the number of birds they had killed in 'hundreds' and big game by the 'score'. Special competitions were arranged in which pigeons were wiped out in colossal numbers. Fortunately this slaughter aroused public opinion and clay pigeon shooting was substituted, the targets being circular discs, and this is now recognized as an Olympic Games event. Another popular modern sport is target shooting. Britain's National Rifle Association was instituted as long ago as 1859, and held its first shoot on Wimbledon Common in 1860. In America, the National Rifle Association is so powerful that it can defeat any proposed legislation to limit the sale and possession of firearms. The indiscriminate slaughter of birds and other wild animals is now frowned upon and severely restricted in an age which at last realizes that wildlife is in danger of extinction. Naturally there are loopholes. The motto of the worst brand of amateur hunter seems to be 'if it moves, shoot it', and on this principle innocent people as well as animals are likely to be casualties in the hunting season.

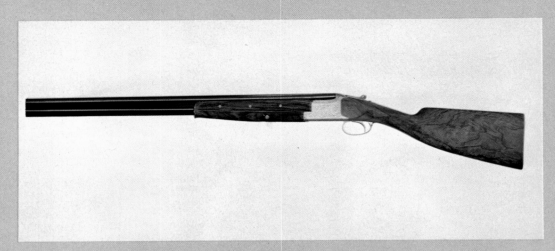

Left The Browning game model shotgun is becoming increasingly popular, and this over-and-under version is of top quality. Great attention has been paid to the engraving, and, although a full coverage, it is indisputably tasteful and well-executed. *Below* The Germans were masters of firearms ornamentation, and this sporting rifle, typical of the first half of the 18th century, is no exception. It was made by J. C. Stockmar of Suhl and has delicately chiselled steel mounts, with a gold background. The elegant stock is decorated with a fine, though restrained, rococo carving. *Bottom* This superb sporting rifle, made for

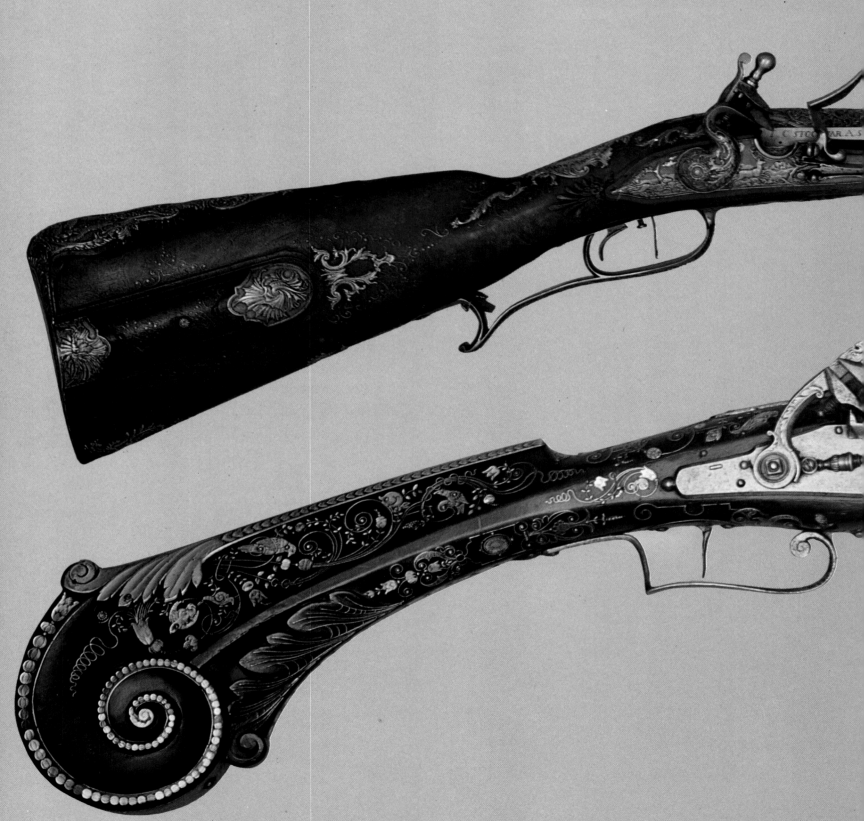

Louis XIII by Pierre le Bourgeoys of Lisieux *c.* 1615, is one of the most beautiful guns of its period. The stock is inlaid silver scroll work, which is also engraved; and the stockmaker has added floral decoration to the butt. The contrasting plain lock plate somehow adds to the overall elegance. *Right* In the world of the shotgun, British weapons still hold their own, both in quality and workmanship. There are numerous makes that cater for sportsmen of modest means, in addition to expensive, custom-made weapons such as this excellent double-barrelled 12-bore 'Royal' model from the world-famous firm of Holland and Holland.

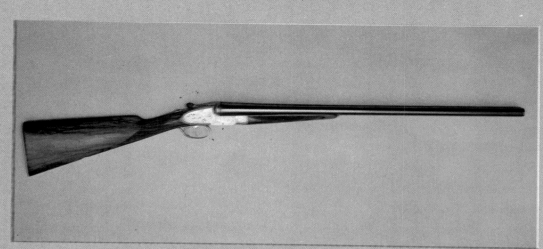

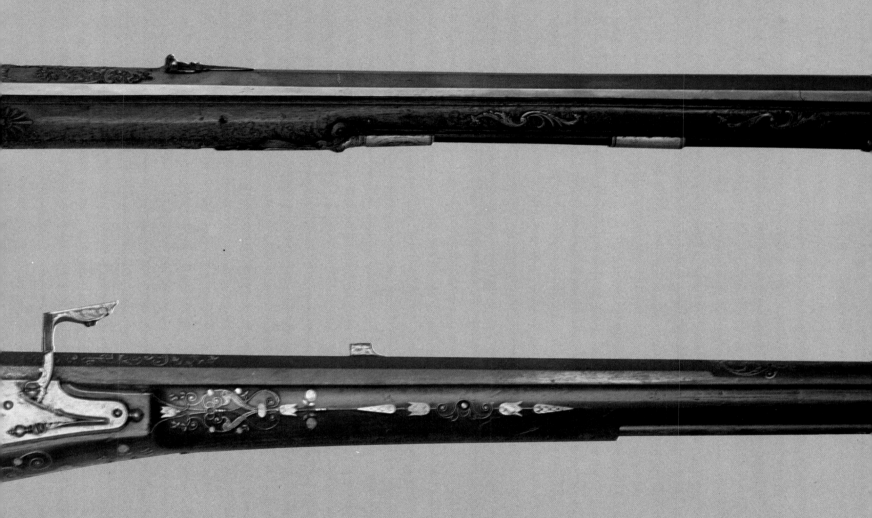

Left The name Mauser has been associated with military and sporting weapons for many years, the firm's first rifles appearing in the 1880s. Here is a close-up of the sighting equipment of a Mauser big game rifle. This gun is fitted with the traditional bolt action that has proved so effective.

Right Big game rifles still exert fascination, even in an age when conservationists insist that there must be strict control over the killing of certain species. Obviously a large-calibre gun is needed to bag a lion, tiger or 'rogue' elephant. This is the Weatherby game rifle with a telescopic sight, a favourite safari weapon.

Below Although the basic appearance of the shotgun has remained unchanged for the last hundred years new features have continually been incorporated or older ones revised. Made by the Etablissements Darne of Saint-Etienne, the breech of this model slides back and incorporates a selective ejector instead of the normal hinged barrels.

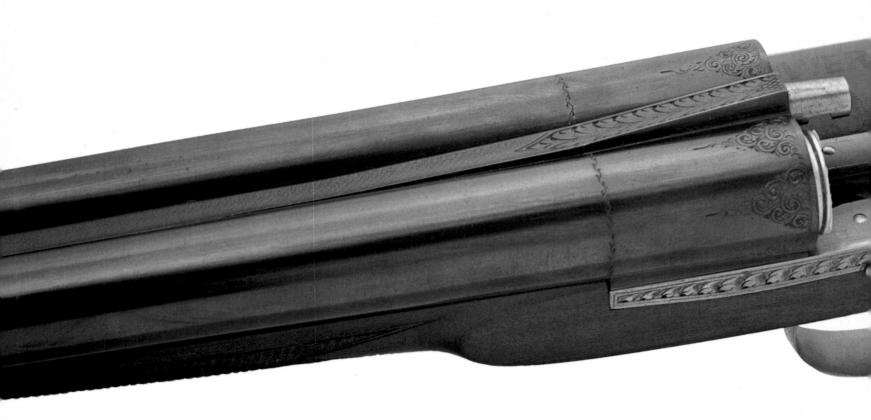

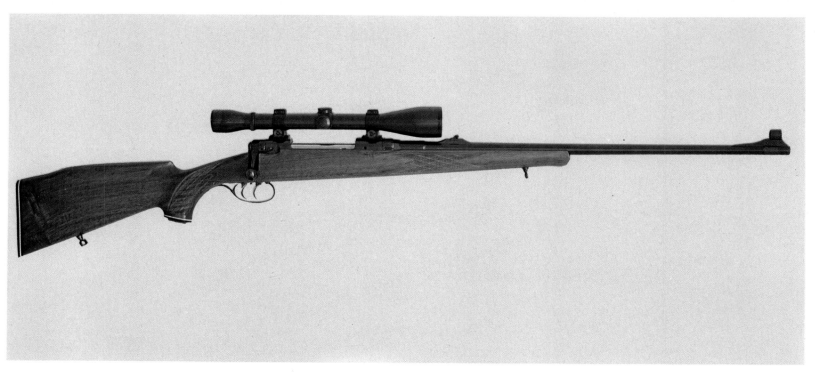

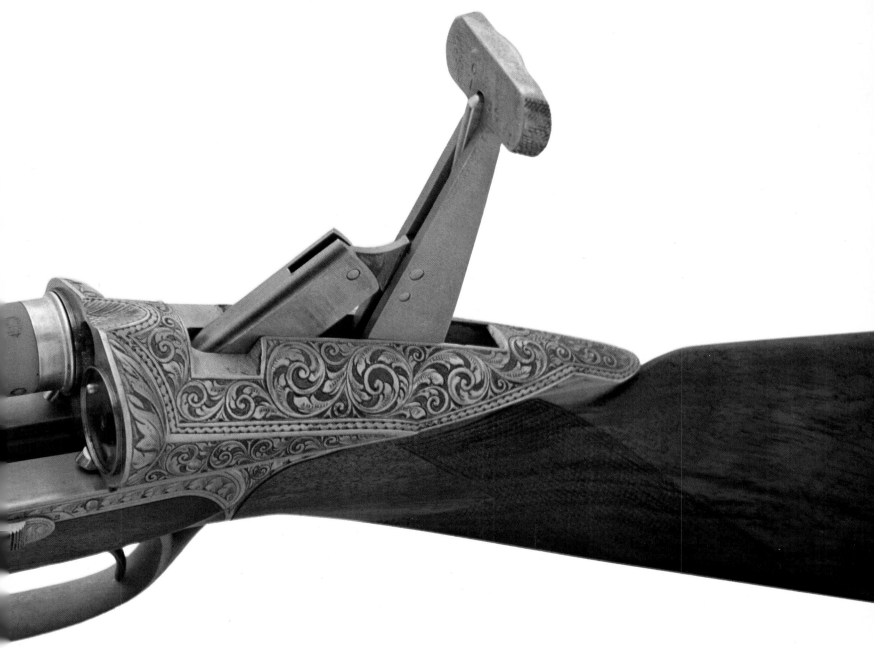

The Rifle

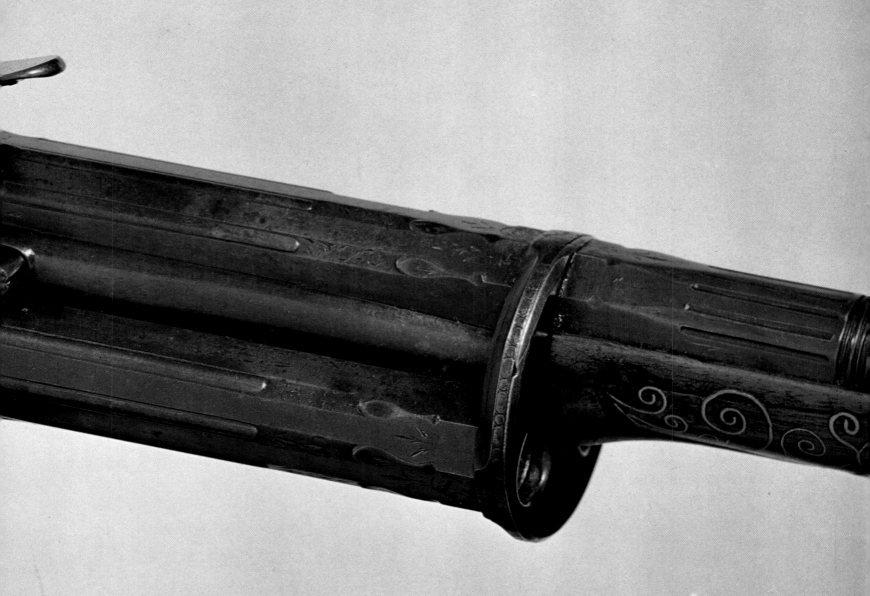

The inventor who first realized that a spinning ball travels straighter and hits harder than one that does not turn was something of a genius. It will come as no surprise to readers that we do not know his name, but it is thought that he lived in Central Europe around 1500. Crossbowmen had offset their bolts to put spin on them in order to make them more accurate, and at some stage an anonymous gunmaker attempted to do the same thing. A rifled gun, believed to have been a snapping matchlock, was apparently owned by Emperor Maximilian I (1459–1519), the 'foremost knight of the age'.

Today, nearly all long guns, except shotguns, are rifled, i.e. spiral-grooved, but the terminology has only been in use for less than 200 years. Before the mid-eighteenth century most shoulder arms were smoothbore and were generally called muskets or 'musquets'. But by the early years of the nineteenth century things were changing fast. In place of the smoothbore arms, an increasing number of guns were made with spiral grooves running from the breech to the muzzle. Technically, these are 'lands' and 'grooves', the lands forming part of the original bore while the grooves or spirals are the actual rifling. The amount of spin given to the bullet when it leaves the gun is dependent on how many there are to a barrel and how many turns there are in its complete length.

The theory of rifling had been studied in many quarters since the

ABOVE *An incident during one of the more obscure 'little wars' of the 19th century, when a British contingent organized by the East India Company, dislodged a Persian force that had occupied the town of Herat in Afghanistan (1856–7). The picture shows Captain J. A. Wood of the 20th Native Infantry winning the Victoria Cross at the storming of Reshire Fort. Commanding Indians armed with .577-calibre Enfield muzzle-loading rifles, Wood was hit by seven musket bullets at point-blank range.*

PREVIOUS PAGES *Many and ingenious were the attempts to produce multi-load firearms, and this fascinating example is one of the better ones. Made in France towards the end of the 17th century, the gun was designed to fire three shots from one loading. Each chamber was loaded with shot and powder, and the pan attached to the chamber was also primed. Once loaded, the breech was turned, so that one of the chambers was in line with the barrels and the hammer cocked.*

early years of the eighteenth century, for by then it was obvious that projectiles from a smooth bore were less steady in the air than from a rifled one. In 1742, the English mathematician and gun expert, Benjamin Robins, wrote: 'the projectile follows the sweep of the rifles [rifling]; and thereby, besides its progressive motion, acquires a circular motion around the axis of the piece, by which means the bullet discharged from a rifle barrel is constantly made to whirl around an axis coincident with the lines of its flight.'

The Germans were among the first to adopt rifled weapons, the previously-mentioned Jaegers being classic examples. However, together with their weight, these weapons had loading problems. To get maximum efficiency, the balls had to be slightly oversize and literally hammered into the rifling. The damage that was often caused in this way, as well as the problem of fouling from burnt powder, necessitated frequent swabbing and cleaning, so that a more efficient means of loading had to be found. Perhaps the most important, and certainly the most effective solution to the problem, was the patched ball, a system that had been in use as early as the sixteenth century. The name of the man who originated the idea is yet another mystery, but the invention was simple and ingenious. In practice, a ball or bullet, smaller than the bore was wrapped in a greased patch of cloth or leather, and rammed down on top of the powder. When the gun was fired, the explosion forced the patch into the rifling and this spun the bullet on its way.

Early German immigrants to what was later Pennsylvania brought with them the Jaeger rifle, and from this was developed the so-called Kentucky rifle of the Revolutionary War. Its original home is thought to have been in Lancaster County, Pennsylvania, where a number of German gunsmiths were known to have settled. Whereas the Jaeger had been primarily a sporting weapon, the new rifle was designed to meet the needs of frontiersman and hunter alike. Most were produced in small calibres from .30 to .45, but some were made with bores as high as .80. The weight was considerably reduced, and the streamlined appearance made it very distinctive. Known by several other names – 'Pennsylvania', 'American', 'Long rifle' – it was as the 'Kentucky' that it won renown. It was held in high esteem by those who used it and was feared by troops who had to face it, such was its accuracy at long distance. But there is no truth in the story that British troops in America refused to advance against soldiers armed with Kentuckys, or that the reputation of the rifle had an adverse effect on recruiting. The fact was that the Kentucky, although in most respects superior to the Brown Bess, took longer to load. For this reason the majority of American troops using them were confined to skirmishing and sniper roles, while the other troops who formed the Continental Army, were armed with Besses or Charleville muskets imported from France. So much for the myth that the Kentucky was the secret weapon which turned the tide against the British.

The Americans were not alone in developing new ideas. A breech loading rifled musket was the invention of a Scotsman from Aberdeenshire, Captain Patrick Ferguson. His design owed something to the earlier work of the Frenchman, Isaac de la Chaumette, but his improvements made the weapon far more practical. A threaded plug attached to the trigger guard was turned down, exposing the breech. Into this were poured powder and ball, and the trigger guard was turned up and locked into position. Then the gun was primed and fired in the normal way. In trials at Woolwich before the assembled Top Brass of the day, and despite rain and high wind, Ferguson hit a target 200 yards away six times in a minute, and proceeded to advance, firing four shots per minute. He concluded the demonstration by hitting the 'bullseye at 100 yards, lying with his back on the ground . . .'

The Board of Ordnance was so impressed that orders were given to supply 100 Fergusons to the Army in America. Others were made for the East India Company. Despite the real success of the rifles in America, however, interest in them lapsed after Ferguson's death at King's Mountain in October, 1780. Several reasons have been given for the failure to exploit a brilliant idea – that the stock was too weak where the breech plug was housed; that the operation of the rifle required unaccustomed skill; that standard cartridges could not be used; that the expense of production was too great; that the weapon was too far advanced for its time – but it remains incomprehensible. What Ferguson had certainly done was to establish the fact that breechloaders would replace guns loaded via the muzzle.

Ferguson's rifle had many successors. In the United States, John Hall was one of several who produced a breechloader; and in Switzerland, Samuel Johannes Pauly also invented one, his innovation being ammunition in the form of an expanding cartridge case, which sealed off the escape of flame and gases. Pauly was followed by his Prussian protégé, Johann von Dreyse, whose experiments at a percussion-cap factory, of which he was part-owner, led to two successes – the famous 'needle gun' in the 1820s and a breechloader in 1837. The Dreyse system was a lead bullet hollowed out to take a primer in its base. This was exploded by a long needlelike firing pin, which passed right through the powder charge and struck the primer. In Europe, the Prussians adopted the new weapon in 1848, trying to keep its construction a secret. So successful were they that the rifle was instrumental in their victory over the Danes in 1864 and their rout of the Austrians in 1866.

In France, the rush to compete with and improve upon the Prussian breechloaders led to the adoption of Antoine Alphonse Chassepot's bolt-action rifle. With its shorter and improved firing pin, this became the standard French weapon for many years and was widely copied.

Until the 1850s, Britain was still recovering from the age of the flintlock, thanks to the arch-conservative Duke of Wellington, who believed that the Brown Bess was the best weapon for infantry. So it was not until the Crimean War that the percussion rifle was wholly accepted by military authorities. By this time the famous Enfield rifles of 1851 and the legendary Pattern 1853 were making their presence felt. As early as 1855 the British Government had bought a number of Sharps' breechloading carbines (these were percussion arms) for cavalry use, but it was not until the 1860s that the true breechloader was officially adopted. Among the many versions tried out were weapons made by Leetch, Prince and Terry. Finally, the action by an American named Jacob Snider was adopted.

Change was in the air. The rimfire cartridge proved reliable and was used by many arms makers, particularly in the American Civil

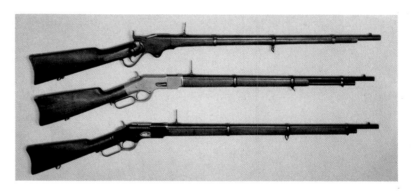

Three famous 19th century rifles. At the top is the seven-shot .52-calibre Spencer of American Civil War fame. The trigger guard was depressed to eject spent cases, and, when closed, fed a fresh round into the breech from a magazine or tube contained in the butt. This held seven copper-cased cartridges. In the centre is the Winchester rifle, model of 1866. It had an all-brass frame and was very popular in the West and as a military weapon. The lower weapon is the full-stocked military version of the legendary Wincheser '73.

War. This was a copper or brass case containing bullet and powder, the base of which was covered with a fulminate. Modern .22 ammunition is identical to that of the 1860s. Although percussion rifles, muskets and revolvers were the main weapons of the Civil War, the breechloading arms of the Sharps, the Spencer (a seven-shot weapon) and others were joined by the new Henry rifle, a sixteen-shot rimfire that was replaced in 1866 by the Winchester.

The first Winchester was a great success on the Plains, and in 1873 came perhaps the most famous rifle of them all, the Winchester '73, often called 'The Gun that Won the West'. It does not deserve all the credit, but its rapid fire was certainly an important factor. On that hot June day in 1876 when General Custer and his entire command were wiped out at the Little Big Horn, a few Winchester '73s might have prolonged the battle, though it would not have affected the result. As it was, too many of the men fought with defective Springfield carbines which jammed and got overheated.

As the guns improved, so did the ammunition. Rimfire gave way to centre-fire, still in use today. The case is made of drawn brass tube, at the bottom of which is placed the cap or primer. By the 1880s, having progressed from earlier forms made of paper and skin (animal entrails), the cartridge, now made of metal, had reached perfection. In fact today's cartridges are almost unchanged.

Left This de luxe model of the Ferguson breech-loading rifle was made by Durs Egg for the Prince of Wales, later King George IV, in 1782. The barrel and lock are inlaid with gold; it has a set trigger and a silver escutcheon.

Top right This Ferguson rifle is of the style described as an 'officer's rifle', because of its military form and the quality of its workmanship. The guard has been turned down so that the breech is exposed, and can be seen from the hole between the hammer and the open pan. Specimens of these rifles are now very rare, and remain in private hands.

Centre right The Kentucky (also known as the American, Pennsylvania or Long) rifle was renowned for its reliability and accuracy. This fine example is signed by S. Miller and dates from *c.* 1810. The maple stock blends well with the ornate brass patchbox set in the side of the butt. Later, many of the old flintlock Kentuckys were converted to percussion locks and the general shape of the rifle survived until the mid-1840s. Surprisingly, some Kentuckys were made in Liège for export, complete with American names–somewhat confusing for collectors.

Bottom right When the Corps of Riflemen (later the Rifle Brigade) was established in Britain in 1800, it was decided to adopt the rifle patented by Ezekiel Baker, the Whitechapel gunsmith. The specimen illustrated is a Volunteer Baker rifle by Wallis and was made *c.* 1810. The rifle was manufactured in several variations and by a number of different makers. Such was its popularity that some British Colonial regiments were armed with it as late as the eighth Kaffir War of 1850–3.

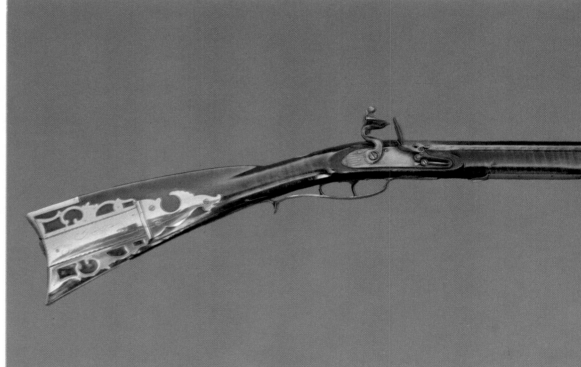

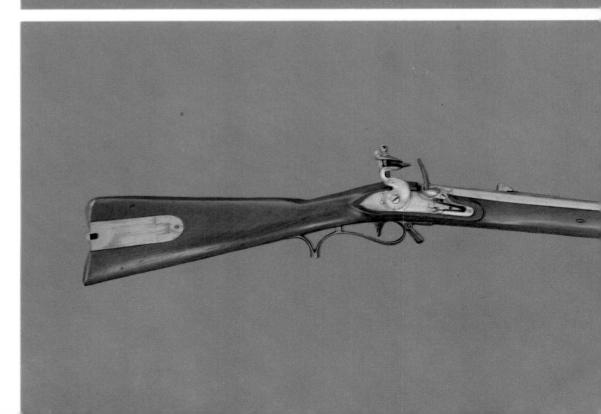

Left The Enfield Pattern 1853 .577-calibre rifle was perhaps the finest percussion muzzle-loader of its day. It was used in four major wars within ten years, including the American Civil War, when many thousands of Enfields were bought by both Confederate and Union forces. Illustrated (top to bottom) are a standard three-band Enfield; a Snyder conversion to cartridge, *c.* 1867; and, for comparison, a German Jaeger type percussion rifle, as developed from the earliest flintlocks that were imported into the United States.

Below The pinfire system of ignition developed by the Frenchman, Casimir Lefaucheux in the late 1820s, became very popular on the Continent. Specimens of such weapons were on display at the Great Exhibition in London in 1851, but the pinfire was never really liked in Britain. This specimen is a pinfire shotgun with a nicely shaped stock and carved cheek-piece.

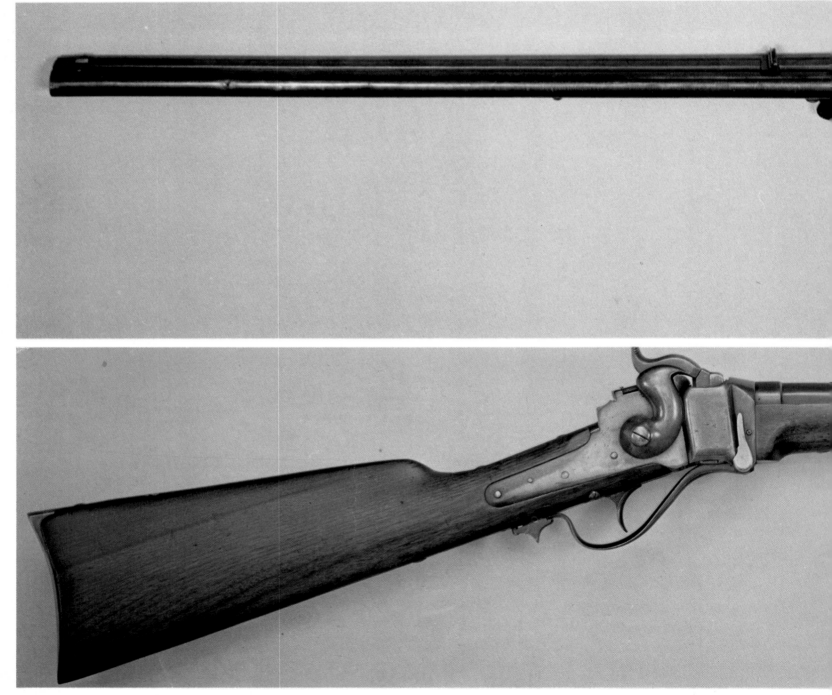

Bottom The American firm of Sharps has for many years produced fine rifles. Some 6,000 of Christian Sharps' early breechloaders were bought by the British Government in 1855, but the boom came in the American Civil War. The gun illustrated is the New Model of 1863, made at lower cost by omitting the patchbox and several accessories. These .52-calibre 22-in barrelled weapons were very popular.

Right At the top of this group is the Lebel 8mm bolt-action rifle, model of 1886, and in the centre is the Dandestean 6.5 carbine model of 1895. Compare these two with the lower weapon, the famous Remington Rolling block action single-shot, in the carbine version. Many thousands of these .43-calibre weapons were sold to the Middle East and some to Europe. The hammer is drawn back to half-cock and the small lever seen just in front of it controls the breech. When pulled back, it ejects a spent case and allows the loading of a fresh one.

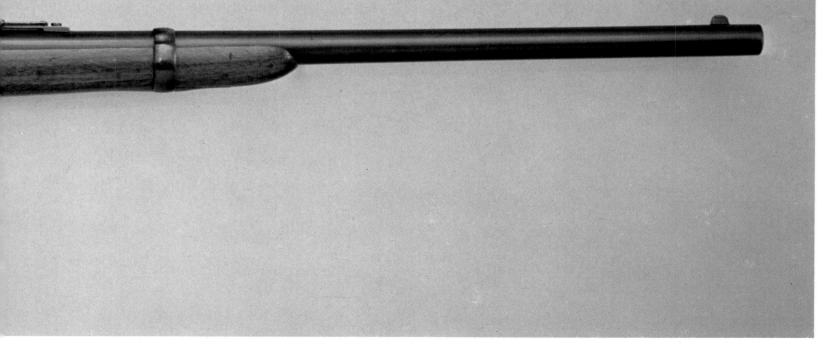

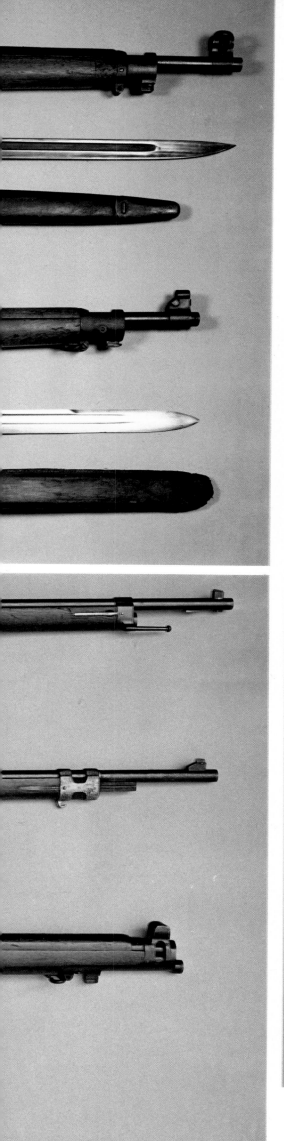

Left When the United States entered World War I in 1917, her service rifle was the Springfield .300 Model 1903 (below). Production of the .303 Model P '14 for Great Britain was well under way, so, with only slight re-tooling, the American version of the P '14 became the Model '17 in .300 calibre (above). The bayonet shown with the Model '17 is familiar to most veterans of Britain's Home Guard and to troops who fought the Japanese in World War II. The 6-in bayonet then in use proved too short to compete with the longer Japanese bayonets and rifles, so the 1917 version was recalled to active service.

Below left These World War I rifles are all basically similar. At the top is the French 8mm Lebel model of 1886, with an internal magazine. The same system is evident with the second rifle, which is the German 7.92mm Mauser Model 98 (Gewehr 98). At the bottom is the famous British .303 S.M.L.E. Mark II (Short, Magazine, Lee-Enfield Mark II).

Below The bolt action which replaced lever action and other systems by the late 19th century led to many variations on the same theme. The illustrations from the left are: Canadian Mark Ross Mark III .303 rifle; the Mark II; a Lee Enfield Mark I; and a Pattern P14. Note that the magazine in front of the trigger guard is common to all. This holds ten rounds, which are loaded and ejected by the action of the bolt.

Rapid Fire

When 5,000 Matabele warriors launched a series of charges on a small British square of some 50 men and were slaughtered in their thousands, a new era in the history of warfare had begun. We are not concerned here with questions of morality, simply to record the fact that on one bloody day in 1893 the Maxim gun made its deadly debut.

By the mid-nineteenth century, firearms had reached a state of sophistication that would have amazed gunsmiths living at the turn of the century, and perhaps have terrified the original matchlock and wheel-lock makers. But there were many who were convinced that guns had not yet reached their acme. Their thoughts turned to mechanical or machine-operated firearms.

Strangely, they were covering old ground. Various types of repeating guns, some very odd and quite impractical, but others more soundly realistic, had been turned out since the sixteenth century. One such invention, which actually received a Board of Ordnance trial, was the so-called 'Puckle's Machine Gun'. Brainchild of a London notary, James Puckle, and patented in 1718, it consisted of a single barrel to which was attached a cylinder containing a number of chambers. The cylinder was revolved by hand but had a handle on the rear which was used to screw the chamber up to the barrel. The mouth of each chamber was coned and fitted into the countersunk breech of the barrel to form a gastight joint. Contemporary reports claim that one man 'discharged it 63 times in seven Minutes, though all the while Raining; and that it throws off either one large or sixteen Musquet Bullets at every discharge with very great Force'. The inventor, clearly of a religious bent, even offered to supply each gun with cylinders that fired round balls against Christians and square ones against Infidels or Turks!

Puckle's gun was not, of course, a true 'machine gun', and neither was another famous weapon, the Gatling. The invention of Dr Richard Gatling, it first appeared in 1862, and is thought to have been demonstrated to Abraham Lincoln. Adopted by the U.S. Government in 1866, it was a multi-barrelled weapon of various calibres (some as large as .58) and the barrels were turned by hand crank. The rate of fire was about 200 rounds per minute, and later 1,500.

The Gatling (which inspired Newbolt's immortal line, 'The Gatling's jammed and the Colonel's dead') was followed by other repeating guns, notably the Hotchkiss, which was used lethally against Big Foot's band of Sioux at Wounded Knee in 1890. However, the Maxim was the real breakthrough. Hiram S. Maxim, an American turned Briton, got the idea when his shoulder was bruised by the recoil of a gun whilst target shooting. He wondered whether the recoil force that produced his bruise could be used to operate a firearm effectively. To be 'automatic' meant that the gases from the discharge of the first round were employed to cock and fire the weapon for the next shot. His conjecture was right. A semi-automatic weapon is one in which a preceding shot can be used to cock the gun but it is only fired by pressure on the trigger.

Progress, after Maxim's discovery, was rapid. John M. Browning produced a fully automatic machine gun for Colt's; the British produced the Vickers and Lewis guns, while on the Continent great strides were being made by a number of companies. By World War I, the machine gun was an integral part of most armies, though the more conservative generals underrated it. The slaughter of the British Army by the Germans on 1 July 1916, the first day of the Battle of the Somme, clinched the matter. A frontal attack in daylight against barbed wire and machine guns was a passport to death.

In addition to machine guns, smaller automatic weapons were developed. A 'recoil operated' revolver was invented by George V. Fosbery and made by the Webley Company, but automatic revolvers were still rarities. It was the true semi- and fully automatic pistols that had the experts thinking in the closing years of the nineteenth and beginning of the twentieth centuries.

PREVIOUS PAGES *One of the most famous light machine guns used by the British Army in World War II was the .303 Bren Light Machine Gun, which proved extremely accurate. Here is a cutaway version, showing the mechanism. Note how the spring in the magazine keeps ammunition at a continuous pressure.*

ABOVE *New Guinea saw some of the bitterest fighting of World War II. The picture, by Ivor Hele, shows a particularly fierce engagement, which occurred on 28 July 1943. The Japanese held a position called old Vickers on Bobdubi Ridge against two assaults by the Australians. Before the third attempt they*

France, Germany and America all worked on the problem. From Germany came two of the most successful, the Mauser and the Luger. The Mauser 1898, commonly called the 'Broomhandle', was a particular favourite of Winston Churchill's, who carried one when charging with the 21st Lancers at Omdurman. Georg Luger's pistol, even more famous, was first produced in 1900. Since that time it has been copied and bought under licence in many European countries, including Britain. It was widely used by the Germans up to and during World War II and still is in constant demand today.

From Japan came the Nambu, which in various forms was a great favourite with her forces in both World Wars. The pistols of Pietro Beretta are generally regarded as Italy's finest achievement in this field, and have an honoured place in fiction. America's many contributions included the legendary Colt-Browning model of 1911, a .45-calibre pistol which has seen service in every war since that date.

All manner of refinements have been added to modern weapons, including silencers. Despite the fact that it is virtually impossible to silence a revolver, because of the lack of a gas seal between the chamber mouth and the barrel breech, fiction writers and film-makers continue to depict their heroes and villians with silenced revolvers, when in fact they should be equipped with automatic pistols! They are on safer ground when they have their gangster heroes of the 1920s and 1930s blazing away with Tommy guns.

Man has advanced far in his search for the ultimate in firearms. Perhaps in developing conventional arms he has reached perfection in that field. But perhaps too the conventional bullet may in turn be replaced by some other propellant, or even the celebrated 'rays' of science fiction. Only time will tell.

were bombarded by artillery and mortar fire, after which a company of the 58/59th Battalion went in just as the enemy were emerging from their dugouts through lifting mortar smoke. The Australians pressed forward, hurling grenades and firing Brens and rifles.

TOP *Its official designation may be the '.45-in Thompson Machine Carbine', but everyone knows it as the 'Tommy gun'. In military circles the Thompson lasted well into World War II, by which time the familiar drum magazine was interchanged with, or replaced by, box versions.*

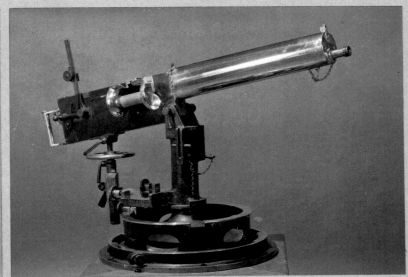

Far left This fine Naval Gatling gun, believe it or not, is basically the same weapon as the one trundled out on wheels by the U.S. Cavalry when faced by hostile Indians. Dr Richard Gatling's gun, not a true machine gun because it is cranked, dates back to the 1860s and has a reliable enough action to have survived to this day. Unlike machine guns proper, the Gatling consists of a cluster of barrels, each fired in turn, which helps cooling. Today's model is the U.S. Air Force Vulcan 20mm, 6-barrel gun, which is capable of firing some 6,000 rounds a minute.

Left Hiram Maxim was an American inventor who became a British knight. In the 1880s he invented the first successful automatic machine gun. This interesting water-cooled version is a later type and exemplifies the development of such weapons.

Right A Vickers-Maxim machine gun in .45-calibre, model of 1894 and one of the oddest of its kind. The mechanism is enclosed, and looks more like an early movie camera than a gun. Nevertheless it was a very lethal weapon.

Below The Lewis Gun illustrated here is a splendid example of a weapon that is still admired by light machine gun buffs. This specimen started life as an aircraft observer's gun, and still retains the spade handle beneath the barrel. Later, a conventional butt, bipod and other refinements were added. Note the drum magazine on top, which is activated by the gun's mechanism.

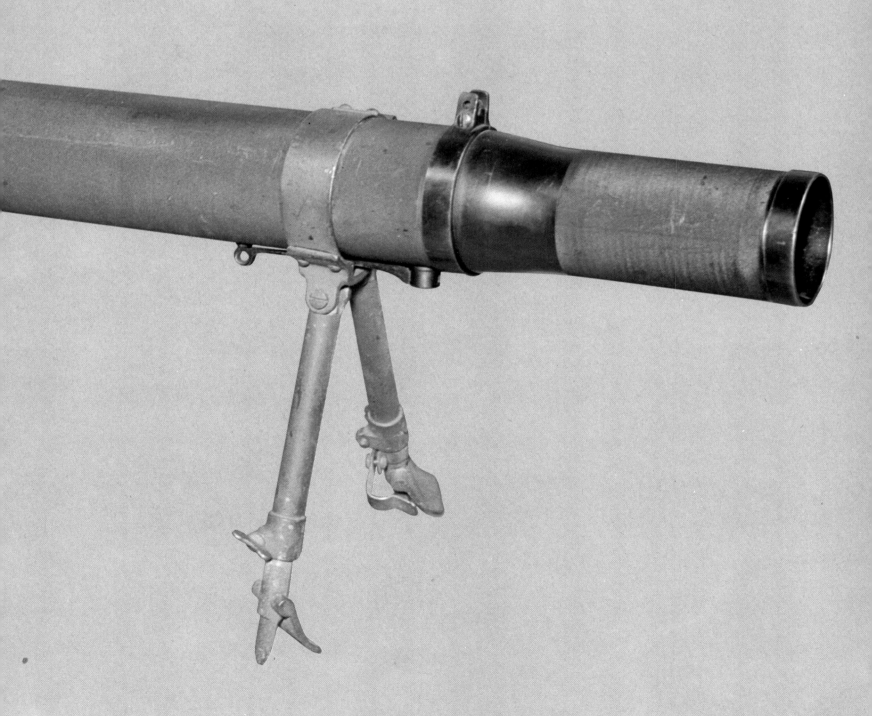

Right This French version of the Hotchkiss machine gun fires its 8mm bullets with lethal effect. The recoil is an unknown quantity, but the gunner's saddle-seat, at the base of the tripod, does not look comfortable.

Far right The Austrian Schwarzloze (or Schwarzlose) medium machine guns, firing 8mm bullets at round 400 rounds per minute, appeared in several versions and were belt-fed. The specimen shown is fitted with open sights, and had a range of about 2,000 metres. Note the racking system to allow maximum elevation.

Below This remarkable and fascinating machine gun is a water-cooled U.R.S.S. Maxim model I, Russian-built weapon, mounted on exceptionally strong wheels designed to stand up to rough terrain. Sighting and elevation are controlled by the movement up and down of the rear sight on its post, and a crank below the gun.

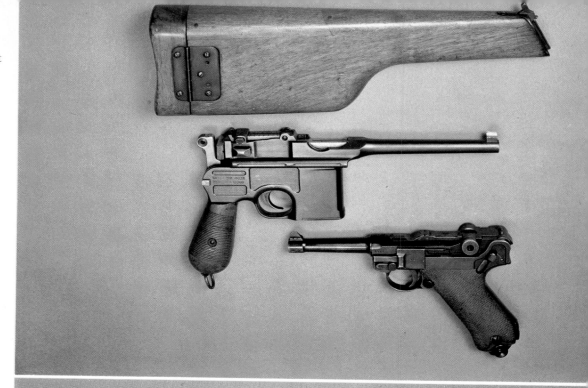

Left The basic function of automatic pistols has not changed during the last 75 years, but they vary a good deal in design. At the top is the Japanese 8mm Nambu Taisho 4. In the centre is the Beretta model of 1934 in 9mm (.380 A.C.P. or Automatic Colt Pistol ammunition), a seven-shot pistol which was very popular and underwent several modifications. At the bottom is the Finnish Lahti 9mm Luger-type pistol.

Top right Germany's two most famous pistols are the Mauser and the Luger. At the top is a splendid Mauser, complete with its unique wooden holster, which also doubles for a carbine stock. The lower weapon is one of the most famous automatic pistols in the world. The basic design owes much to the work of Hugo Borchardt (who worked for a time at the Winchester factory), but it was Georg Luger who made the improvements that led to the weapon being immortalized in his name. (Purists, however, still prefer the term Parabellum to Luger!) Loaded with 8 cartridges in a magazine held within the butt, this 9mm pistol is still eagerly sought by shooters and gun collectors.

Centre right The first Mauser automatic pistol was produced in 1898 in 7.63mm, and young Winston Churchill purchased one of the first to reach Britain. Buffs refer to it as the 'broomhandle' because of the shape of the butt, and when equipped with a stock, which serves as a holster, it is a very effective carbine.

Bottom right John Browning pioneered many automatic pistols and machine guns. Among his early successes, produced while he worked for the Colt Company at Hartford, was the famous 1911 .45 automatic pistol, still the mainstay, with variations, of Colt weapons to this day. This pistol, although manufactured by the Belgian company, Fabrique Nationale (F.N.), closely resembles the original Browning model of 1911, but has undergone refinements. It is known as the 'F.N.-Browning High Power Auto Pistol, calibre 9mm Parabellum'. The high-quality engraving is not, of course, a 'standard issue'!

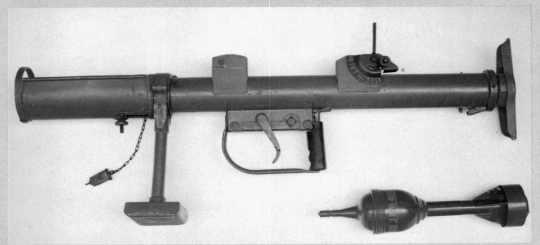

Left The development of effective anti-tank guns has become increasingly important in recent decades. The United States' Bazooka and the British anti-tank rifle were two of the many and later weapons proved equally effective, or were designed to cope with reinforced armourplate. Shown here is a typical anti-tank gun, the P.I.A.T., complete with missile.

Below The Russian P.P.P.S.L.K. submachine gun illustrated at the top is very similar in appearance to the Thompson. Shown below is the German Bergmann 9mm machine carbine. This version is drum-fed, but others were equipped with 32-round box magazines, and had a range of about 1,000 metres.

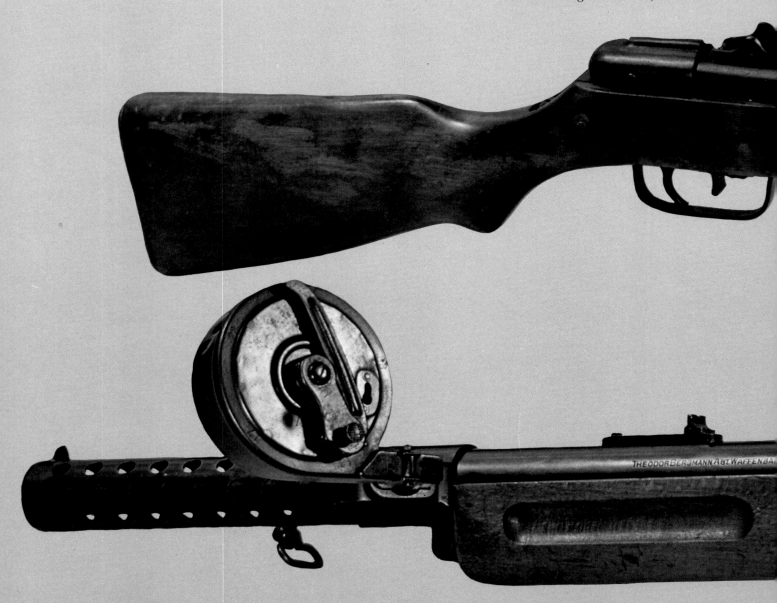

Right The popularity of the Bren gun was
due, apart from its accuracy, to its lightness
and strength. Remarkable too was the ease
with which it could be stripped in the field.
Yet another advantage was its ability to
fire either bursts or a succession of single
shots. Originally of Czech design, its name is
derived from the composite initials *Br*no
(where it was first designed), and *En*field
(the British Small Arms factory where it was
made).

Top left Czechoslovakia, producers of many excellent light machine guns, continues to improve on previous designs. Illustrated at the top is the Scorpion, which has a very distinctive automatic pistol appearance. Shown below is an Israeli Uzi submachine gun that has proved its worth in recent wars.

Below The British Sten Gun, officially designated as the 'Sten Machine Carbine', appeared in several versions. This is the Mark II, fitted with a conventional skeleton stock rather than the straight rod and flat bar common to most of the Mark II and Mark III versions. These robust weapons were capable of a rate of fire of over 500 rounds per minute, depending, of course, on how fast the user could change the 32-round-capacity magazine.

Bottom Although these submachine guns are not as well-known as, say, the Thompson, they are striking in their simplicity. At the top is the Australian Owen, suitably camouflaged, and at the bottom is the Danish Madsen. Notice the position of both magazines.

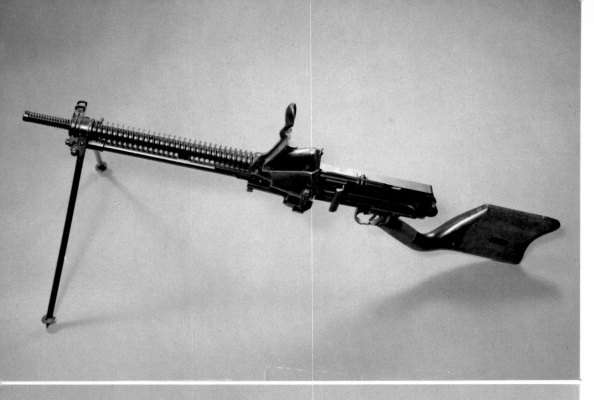

Left It may look weird, but, like most Japanese weapons of war, the Nambu light machine gun was remarkably efficient. Weapons like these, stripped to bare essentials, proved deadly when used in confined spaces or in jungle warfare. The strange, spiral-like effect created on the barrel is to aid cooling.

Below left Colt firearms have turned full circle since 1835 when Samuel Colt first patented his revolver in Britain, and this illustration shows how far design has advanced. At the left is a commercial version of the Colt Armalite. In the centre and right are two military versions of the M16 semi-automatic rifle, used by U.S. forces in Vietnam. The centre rifle is equipped with telescopic sights. A similar weapon has been produced by the company as the 'AR15 Sporter Model Rifle', and is almost identical to its military counterpart. The M16s are produced in .223-calibre (or 5.56mm) and have a magazine capacity of 5, which can be increased to 30 by means of a box magazine, giving a rate of fire of 650–850 per minute.

Index

Page numbers in *italics* refer to captions.

Acknowledgements

The authors and publishers would like to thank the following for their help in the preparation of this book:
Dr A. Borg of the Tower of London Armouries and Mr Hubert Woodend, Curator of Pattern Room, Royal Small Arms Factory, Enfield.

The publishers would like to thank the owners, authorities and trustees of the following collections and museums for their kind permission to reproduce the illustrations in this book:

Gracious Permission of Her Majesty the Queen (Windsor Castle): 74
Armee Museum, Ingolstadt: 16–17 top
Australian War Memorial, Canberra: 82–83
Bayerisches Nationalmuseum, Munich: 66–67 centre
Carlo Bevilacqua: 4–5, 10–11 bottom, 12 below right, 14, 32 top right, 86–87 bottom, 87 top, 89 centre, 90 top, 91 top, 92–93
British Museum: 8–9, 38, 64, 65
F. N. Browning: 66 top, 89 below
Christies: 24 top, 34 bottom
Nino Cirani: 68 top, 69 top
Connecticut State Library Museum (photo Gus Johnson): 51 all
Cooper-Bridgeman Library: endpapers, 25 top, 32 top left, 32–33, 41 bottom, 58–59, 76–77 bottom
Department of the Environment (Crown copyright reserved): 8 above, 28 top and centre
John Freeman: 16–17 bottom, 18–19 top, 25 bottom, 26–27, 34 top
Thomas Gilcrease Institute of American History and Art: 48
Gower Guns: 68–69
Sonia Halliday Photographs: 13
Michael Holford: 12 left, 65
Holland & Holland: 67 top
Angelo Hornak: 2–3, 20–21, 22 top, 26 above, 28 bottom, 29, 30 right, 31, 36–37, 40–41, 41 top, 42–43, 43, 44 bottom, 45, 46–47, 49, 50, 54 top, 54–55, 55 top, 56, 58 above and bottom, 59 top, 61 top, 61 bottom left, 73, 76 top, 76–77 top, 80–81, 82 top, 84 top left and right, 84–85, 88, 89 top, 90–91, 92 top, 93 bottom, 94 both, all jacket pictures
Jago Museum: 10–11 top, 24 centre and bottom, 70–71
W. Keith Neal: 39, 52–53 top and bottom, 75 centre and bottom
Edwin Meyer, Vienna: 15 top, 35
Museo Artiglieria, Turin: 16–17 centre
National Army Museum: 42 top right, 52 left, 72
National Museum of Antiquities of Scotland: 27 top
Phoebus Picture Library: 1, 15 centre right, 60, 61 centre and bottom, 77 top, 78 top and bottom, 79, 86–87 top
Poldi Pezzoli Museum, Milan: 6–7
Private Collection, 2–3, 22 top, 26 above, 28 bottom, 29, 30 right, 31, 41 top, 42–43, 43, 44 bottom, 45, 50, 54, 61 bottom left
T. H. Porter: 30 left
Quebec House, Westerham, Kent (National Trust, photo Eileen Tweedy): 22–23 below
Royal Armoury, Turin: 10 left both
Royal Scottish Museum: 18–19 bottom, 33 top, 75 top
Royal Small Arms Factory, Enfield: 49, 55 top, 61 top, 80–81, 82 top, 84 left and right, 84–85, 88, 90–91, 92 top, 93 bottom, 94 both, jacket front flap
Scala: 6–7, 10 left both, 16–17 centre
Smith & Wesson: 57 both

Smithsonian Institution, Washington, D.C.: 44 top, 4¼″ barrel, cal. 45: Donor–Supreme Council Scottish Rites; 3″ barrel, cal. 45: Donor–Major Gen. John R. Brook; 2″ barrel: Donor–Miss L. Boyd; 3″ barrel: cal. 50: Donor–William Perrow)
Sothebys: 15 bottom right, 42 top left, 62–63, 66–67 bottom
Tower of London Armouries (Crown copyright–reproduced with permission of Her Majesty's Stationery Office): front and back and back flap of jacket, endpapers, 8 above, 15 centre right, 20–21, 25 top, 28 top and centre, 32 top left, 32–33, 41 bottom, 46–47, 54 top, 56, 58 above and bottom, 58–59, 59 top, 73, 76 top, 76–77 bottom, 89 top
Victoria & Albert Museum: 27 centre, 36–37, 40–41
Vickers Ltd: 85 top
Wadsworth Atheneum, Hartford, Connecticut (Colonel Samuel Colt Collection); 12 above right, 18–19 centre
Wallace Collection (Crown copyright reserved) 15 below left, 16–17 bottom, 18–19 top, 25 bottom, 26–27, 34 top

Jacket illustrations *front*: double-barrelled flintlock sporting gun by Boutet *c.* 1785; flintlock repeating gun constructed on the revolver principle by Manresa, 1739; German ivory priming flask *c.* 1680; *back*: Colt navy revolver 1851; Saxon powder flask *c.* 1600; Russian flintlock gun dated 1752; German wheel-lock steel pistol; Dutch matchlock musket *c.* 1620; small Spanish automatic *c.* 1920.

M.346E.194L